Love Yourself for no Reason!

Self-rejection is a prison.
Here is your escape plan.

Mark Peter Kahn

First Edition December 2016
ISBN: 978-1-920535-97-1

Author's website: www.loveyourselffornoreason.com

www.kwarts.co.za

DEDICATION

To all of us who have suffered because we do not feel good enough as we are. Right here, right now!

Before we have done anything, achieved anything, proved anything.

Forever gazing into the distance, toward that misty blue horizon, looking again for the next thing, the next person, the next achievement that will save us from this persecuting voice that says we are just not good enough as we are now.

The tortured cry which says:

"I'm not a good enough mother, I'm not a good enough father or partner or son or daughter, or contributor to society. I'm not successful enough, I haven't made enough money, my body is too fat or too thin or ugly. I am too selfish, too opinionated, so irritable, so unfocused, such a procrastinator, so undisciplined, so angry and critical. My mind is so restless and incessantly thinking insane and mundane thoughts."

To all of us, may we be blessed to know the truth and joy and love that we are.
Right here.
Right now.

In Love and Power,
Mark

REVIEWS

Over the years my appetite for self-help books has waned in direct proportion to their unhelpfulness. Under invitation I sat at my kitchen counter and started to read Mark Peter Kahn's *Love yourself for no reason*. I noticed I wanted to read on; my thoughts and feelings were stimulated, stirred and more significantly, stilled. The substance of this book lies in the author uniting a trilogy of decades of personal processing, innumerable hours of working with others, alongside years of rigorous research.

It is in the alchemy of Mark's personal journey, his keen observation of others and passion for experimentation and exploration that *Love yourself for no reason* has been forged. The author expresses a united voice of journeyman, facilitator and scientist, creating a book that is personal with public reach, a work that in its witnessing shows the way and literature that offers a recipe you can taste.

Love yourself for no reason offers a diagnostic truthfulness that creates resonance with the reader. The book illustrates a deep appreciation of complexity avoiding a superficial, reductionistic approach. And its ultimate intrigue and success rests in the presentation of Love without reason.

Natalie Uren. Author of:
The Purple Egg & co-author of Food does not make you fat.

Self-love. It's a magical power. As a therapist of many years I've been witness to the results that self-love can bring in completely changing a person's life around.

In *Love yourself for no reason,* Mark Peter Kahn thoughtfully dispels the myth that the way to feel good is to have good things happen to us. Instead he shows the reader that feeling good comes from an internal power, the power of love.

He discusses how much of the time we disconnect from our internal power, evidenced by the self-sabotaging ways we think, our need for perfection and our fear of being judged.

In this deeply compelling book Mark Peter Kahn looks at the difference between Acquired Self-Esteem, that which we learn through approval, and Original Self-Esteem which is our authentic pure consciousness – this is when we are in flow when we are connected and empowered.

There are a number of very helpful techniques and practices designed to aid the reader in letting go of their Acquired Self-Esteem and to be able to begin finding their internal power by connecting with their Original Self-Esteem. The power of love.

A well written, easy to follow yet thought-provoking book that you will want to read more than once!

Marlene Rose Shaw
Author of: Out Of Fear Into Love: Life doesn't have to be a struggle.

Love yourself for no reason is a practical and inspiring book written with insight and wisdom. Clinical psychologist Mark Peter Kahn's book will be life-changing for anyone suffering from Self-Esteem issues. The book offers empowering help for those living in the hell of "I'm not good enough". With unique techniques, strategies and meditations, the book provides the answers to healing your pain and learning to "activate love" and internal power that will transform your life.

Lindsey Sanderson
Former senior copy editor of The Star newspaper and short story author.

IN GRATITUDE

To Suzie. Bless you, I love you. You have supported me in immeasurable ways at all levels. Your faith in me and this work has been there always, like the hum of the universe in the background *and* the foreground, sustaining me endlessly. Your resonance, the *energetic signature* of your being-ness, infiltrates everything I do. You are a blessing in my life beyond the telling of it.

To my parents, who didn't give me what I wanted but gave me everything I needed to enable this work to emerge out of me.

To my dear sister Kathy. Thank you for your so consistent and endless support of this work, from that bleak and cold and cloudy home you call, England.

To Adyashanti, who reignited my spiritual quest, there are no words except my open heart.

To Dr Bruce Hoffman, who has helped to keep my body going against all odds – thank you!

To Dr John Demartini, for your great wisdom and psychological insights, none of which are to be found in the psychology textbooks I've read! You separated me from the rigidity of my training. What freedom!

To Nina Twombly. You have helped me to revitalise my energy system. What a blessing you are.

To Kate Reymond, one of the most beautiful and special people I have ever met, who taught me so much about this work and who so sensitively and bravely transformed her life.

To the thousands of people I've met over my lifetime: my clients, my friends, my enemies, those whose books I read, whose movies I watched, everyone who taught me so much. All of you are inside my heart and inside of my mind and you are inside of this work. I bow down before you, I thank you.

FOREWORD

I have known Mark Kahn for the last 10 years. During this period he has attended many of my human behavioural presentations, seminars and trainings. At a particular transition point in his life he began incorporating some of the principles and methodologies that I teach into his personal and professional life. He became one of my first South African Certified Demartini Method facilitators and began transforming the lives of many of his clients through incorporating his previous trainings, his newest understandings as well as some of my own principles and methods.

When I met Mark he was in the process of getting divorced and was moving away from many aspects of the traditional psychological models that were no longer inspiring and that were not achieving what he felt his clients deserved. He soon expanded his understanding and training and modified his approach to that which was more 'method based' and which had more of a spiritual foundation to it. He approached his objective as well as learned my method with the tenacity and commitment that was both touching and very gratifying to observe and work with. Because of his commitment and drive, he gradually developed his own innovative approach to psychology and created what he terms "transition points" and the *Cultivating Wisdom* method, which he found helped transform and spiritually fulfil the lives of his clients.

Due to his many years of effort, it comes as no surprise to me that he was able to create his ground-breaking body of work around Self-Esteem that I believe will make a great contribution to the field of human development and spiritual growth. Now, in his new book, *Love yourself for no reason!*, he expresses his body of work openly, which is in some cases diametrically opposed to the predominant practice throughout the world: "Do what I expect of you and I will love you!"

Our culture is often run through with rules and injunctions designed to get people to fit themselves into boxes which are in many cases a denial of their uniqueness and individuality. Very few people believe that they are "good" enough as they are. It is the conditioning of our culture that suggests, in multiple ways, that we have to become something we are not in order to feel special, worthwhile and lovable.

This insightful book is both a direct and powerful response to the prison walls created by such social conditioning. To dismantle these walls enables a freedom of spirit and psyche to emerge that honours the individuality, the uniqueness and genius of every one of us.

Mark's *Cultivating Wisdom* method is elegant in its simplicity and really powerful in application, in that it addresses how to dissolve the conditioning we sometimes feel has been "inflicted" upon us. Essentially, we have been sold a bill of goods or, in some settings, a bunch of lies, masquerading as truth, which turn us away from our unique talents and magnificence. Mark's book will assist you in breaking through these lies and turning back towards the truth of who you are, to discover the energy and power that resides within, when you honour your true self.

His method for accessing love and power internally can now enable you to appreciate yourself, and allow your specialness and uniqueness to emerge, adding a richness to your life that can make it truly worth living. It is only when we honour our uniqueness that our lives become not just manageable, but deeply rewarding.

Mark's work explores from many angles the ways in which we move into self-doubt and contraction and the alternative path of honouring ourselves, which is expansion. This contraction-expansion model is a great depiction of the energetic nuances that reflect the human struggle to simply ... be ourselves. To just notice this movement between contraction and expansion and to learn to spend more time in the latter opens a doorway into healing and self-love.

The poems he has written throughout the book capture the depth and power of this work, beyond intellectual analysis, beyond mind. They reflect what it means to emerge out of the perceived pain of persecution, generated externally and internally, as a resonant Spirit, into this world that is always both challenging and supporting us. They reflect the agony *and* the healing into self-love and internal power that is deeply gratifying.

To the victim, everything is in the way. To the Master, everything is on the way. If you approach this work with any degree of intent and focus, you will be well *on the way* to self-loving mastery ... for no reason!

Dr. John F. Demartini

PREFACE

The Greatest Three Minutes
of my University Career

If you take the six years I spent at university studying psychology and look at value for time, there were three minutes that overwhelmingly dominated everything else I learned.

And I *really* mean *overwhelmingly.*

It stands out as an inspired "yes!" moment of immense proportions.

It was my introduction to internal power and self-love in interactions with others.

I was in my fifth year. I was doing a role-play with a colleague that was being video-taped. She was the client, I was the therapist.

We walked into the room in which there were two chairs. She chose a chair and sat down and started to talk. My supervisor, Professor Jill Straker, stopped the video recorder when we were replaying it and asked the class: "What just happened?"

We all had four years of psychology theory behind us and we were stumped. And by the way, I have met many people in my coaching and therapy work who answered the question correctly without any psychology background at all, but their years of experience had served them well and they knew.

And the answer to the professor's question was: "Control!"

My colleague who was playing the role of client had taken control of the situation completely. A person who wasn't doing control would have waited to see which chair the therapist offered her and they might have waited for the therapist to introduce themselves.

Now you might think that this is an over-analysis of the situation. Believe me, it's not. This colleague was exactly like that in her life!

When we walked out of a lecture she would have been the first one to say: "Let's go for lunch. There's a lovely fish restaurant up the road." Without asking if anyone else wanted lunch and what they wanted to eat. Control was her middle name.

What's also interesting is that I've done years of role-plays in businesses, running workshops, and people don't like role-plays and they often say they're not representative of real-life. This example disproves their point!

So what is this "yes!" moment of inspiration about?

What was a revelation for me was that for the first time in my life, I saw that in any interaction there are always two levels of meaning operating: the content and the exchange of emotional energy between the parties.

The content is the words. "Hi, my name is Mark." This is simply an introduction.

I'm sharing my name. Content is the details, the operational issues, the meaning of the words. The exchange of energy is the tone, the energetic signature *underlying the words*.

It is about how things are said and how they are being received. What is the energetic tone *between* the parties?

Very few people – except kids – pay any attention to the energetic tone in the relationship between the people.

So kids will meet someone and say: "Mummy, he smells", or "He's fat", or "I don't like being in this house. It feels funny".

In other words, kids are very tuned in to the exchange of energy in relationships and they will verbalise it and then be told to be polite or to simply shut up!

So it is our conditioning that shuts down our spontaneity and most importantly our awareness of what's going on in the relationship.

You walk into a business meeting and somebody just jumps straight into what they're wanting to talk about. You feel disoriented because you haven't established an agenda and they have taken control of the meeting and you're left feeling anxious and uncertain.

Real power is to say: "Hang on a moment. Can we just establish what the agenda is here, before we go on with the point that you're wanting to make?"

People with great Self-Esteem, who have a lot of internal power, are aware of what's going on in the exchange of energy and they can use it to maintain power, improve communication, reduce confusion and resolve conflict. In a world where bad communication and conflict is rife, this is an incredible skill.

Let me share some more examples with you.

You arrive at a holiday home of a friend of yours at the coast. There are many guests staying in the house but they haven't arrived yet. Your host ushers you into the smallest room at the back of the home without a view of the sea. What's happening in the exchange of energy is that you are horrified and resistant to this. To spend five days in this beautiful place in a cubby-hole-of-a-room is deeply distressing.

If you're standing in your power, you say smiling: "Is this the only option for us?"

Many years ago I used to live 25 km north of Johannesburg, South Africa, in a grassland area called the Rhenosterspruit Nature Reserve. ("Renoster" is the Afrikaans word for rhinoceros.)

I was attending a meeting hosted by the West Rand administration board around a lot of the regulations regarding landowners and workers.

The presenter had his PowerPoint running beautifully and was well into his presentation when an uneducated labourer at the back of the room put up his hand and said: "Excuse me sir, but I wonder if you could explain everything in more simple language because we really don't understand you."

There appeared to be no fear in saying, "I don't know what's going on".

And believe me, I had no clue as to what the presenter was saying either, but I was too frightened – with all my degrees and sophistication – to ask!

How much of the time does your fear of looking *stupid* prevent you from opening your mouth and expressing your misunderstanding? The key is in the exchange of energy in the relationship?

In terms of Self-Esteem, this is an absolutely critical issue. People with very low Self-Esteem hardly ever, ever interpret and frame statements or questions around what's going on in interactions.

Which means that their intentions, needs, wants, feelings, desires, perceptions and *creativity* are kept hidden, repressed, denied, squashed excruciatingly down into their gut.

And these unexpressed feelings and wants dissolve their power.

It's like walking around living your life while hiding in a miniature bunker that enshrouds you everywhere you go!

It's not just staying under the radar; it's cowering there, wishing life wasn't so harsh and difficult and threatening.

And what stays under the radar *disempowers* you, because all of that energy is locked up inside. It is not available to influence what is happening. Other people, who aren't disempowered, will then push you around.

In addition, locked-up energy will boil away inside you and that "boiling" energy is really painful to live with *and* it wants to get out! It's imprisoned.

It takes immense energy to keep those prison bars in place.

People with low Self-Esteem are trying to get through life with as little trouble as possible. They are rejecting themselves.

Self-rejection is a prison. This book is your escape plan.

When you reject yourself, you are trying to navigate a safe passage through interactions, which means that you're ignoring one of the two key elements in interactions, which is *what is going on emotionally between people.*

It's always fear that controls us and prevents us from expressing what we think is going on in the interaction. It's a fear of looking stupid. It's a fear of creating conflict and disharmony. It's a fear of looking selfish or pushy and, ultimately, it's wanting to control the perceptions of others.

When you don't have to control what other people think of you, it is paradise found!

This discovery changed my life over 30 years ago. It was my introduction into personal power. I took it to another level when I created this Self-Esteem work.

When you stand resolute, clear and strong in your power, you are *loving yourself!*

And this book is about internal power *and* love.

I will be sharing more stories that reflect how to be more powerful and hence loving, toward yourself, in Chapter 18: Boundaries in action!

My wish for you is that this journey into loving yourself and discovering internal power is a revelation.

Contents

INTRODUCTION

"Your most important job in life is to love yourself for no reason."

It is a crime against humanity how we are taught to judge, malign, abuse and crucify ourselves.

We love kids, before they do anything.

Before they succeed or fail.

Why do we not afford adults the same honour?

You look at a one-year-old child and what do you think?

Pure, unadulterated love.

You just love it for its innocence, its openness, its cuteness, the curiosity and joy in its face. It doesn't have to do anything for you to love it! And it's not just "by the way" that they aren't always innocent and open and curious and cute, is it?

And yet we still love them!

You love them without reserve, without condition.*

We believe children are lovable, just simply as they are, without them having to do anything to earn it or deserve it.

So why on earth, when a child gets to five or six years of age, do they now have to **do** something in order to **deserve** being loved?

They have to perform, to achieve, to succeed before we love them – *and most of us carry this burden to our graves!*

I believe that the way culture conditions us to think that we have to earn love when we are no longer small and that love is only to be given when earned or deserved, is insane.[1]

I believe it is a crime.

Why?

Because most reasonable people are going to tell you that physical and sexual abuse of children is horrific and awful.

And yet the latest research in neurofeedback shows that the effect on the brain of emotional abuse is identical to that of physical and sexual abuse. Which means that when we tell a child that they are not okay and not lovable because they have failed an exam, because they are selfish, because they are "lazy" and don't do their schoolwork, we are changing their brainwave pattern in the same way as physical abuse does, with all of the accompanying physiological and emotional effects.

So the most important and powerful work you can do if you want to improve your Self-Esteem is to heal the wounds created by this abuse, activating self-love and internal power.

That is the core message and method of this book.

Can you love yourself now, for no reason at all?

I'm not really expecting you to be able to do it now, but if you read this book and practise the exercises, that is a distinct possibility.

---

1   There is actually no such thing as unconditional love. Why? Because there would then have to be conditional love, which is a contradiction in terms. If there's a condition attached to a loving feeling, then it can't be love. Love is just love, the word unconditional in front of the word love is superfluous.

The next option is:

Can you love yourself in the face of intense rejection from others?

This is the ultimate test.

When we are sitting alone, reflecting on our lives, it is much easier to love ourselves than when we are confronted by somebody who rejects us, criticises us, maligns us.

If you don't love yourself, then just the slightest criticism from someone else sets up the need to defend and protect your self-image, and the potential for argument and war begins.

Nobody talks about internal power.

I've been a psychologist for over 30 years and I've never had a client arrive at their first session stating their problem as: "I'm short on power", or "I give away my power too easily...", or "I'm easily overpowered".

People don't talk like that. Yet everybody is "underpowered" in varying ways, to some degree. This issue is just not fully recognised or understood.

People often say, "I have a lot of anxiety," or "I'm a pushover." or "I lack confidence." But they're not really getting to the *energetic* core of their problem.

Power and love are at the core of the issue because it all starts with energy in the body and you either have a great deal of energy or you're struggling to find energy. And most people experience a multitude of situations in which they struggle to access love and power, energy in the body.

In this book I intend to rectify this gap in our understanding and I will share with you a magnificent tool designed to enable the acquisition of love and personal power.

Doing this is, for many people, the first step in loving themselves. Living in power is to activate Self-Love.

I say "personal power", because as power has been so abused in our society, we mostly come to think of it as being something that we hold *over* others. Power is what corporations and politicians and parents and teachers hold over us and let's not forget centuries of men's abuse toward women, and as for racism ... I'm not even going to start on that one!

Power over others is really about control and the ability to manipulate, dominate and threaten others.

This is not the kind of power I'm talking about.

I'm discussing an internal power that is experienced physically, as sensations and emotions in the body and which is related to thoughts and belief systems in the mind and in relation to other people and the world, *in behaviour.*

When I talk about power in this book and in this work I'm referring to how you position yourself *energetically,* internally, in relation to success and failure and criticism and doubt and stress and trauma and rejection and sickness and accidents and pain.

I am talking about an *energetic signature* of power: what it looks and feels like and how to acquire it. It is a mental and emotional tone that is vibrant and spirited.

I will use the term *energetic signature* a great deal in this work. It refers to how we appear to the world "energetically", how we position ourselves and come across, as an energy system.

We get people's energetic signature the moment we meet them. It's either timid, shy, retreating, avoidant, anxious, diffident, apologetic, uncertain, hesitant, sweeeet (incorrect spelling intended), disempowered and loveless. Or strong, activated, energised, spirited, commanding, certain, confident, unapologetic, powerful and loving.

This work is about retaining your *energetic signature* of love and power, irrespective of events around and within you.

It's fascinating to notice how we go into a state of shock when unexpected accidents and trauma occur. If somebody close to us dies unexpectedly or gets ill, or we suddenly have an unexpected physical problem, or our kids have an accident or get sick, we usually go into panic and shock, which is a loss of internal power.

In essence, we learn to give away our power to life, to people and events from a very early age.

WHERE DOES HAPPINESS ORIGINATE?

Most people experience happiness as coming from the outside. You get a rebate from the tax man and you are excited, you fall in love and you are ecstatic. You get a raise or start a new career and you feel much happier.

Kids are much better at feeling happy for no reason at all, than adults.

Their happiness is generated internally.

If you don't need others to make you feel good, you are free. The alternative is a prison.

I love asking my adult clients the question, "Can you sing?"

95% of them say no. They are in what I call Acquired Self-Esteem. It is Self-Esteem learned through being approved of. Original Self-Esteem is what we are born with.

Kids are essentially born with a sense of joy and wonderment and curiosity and love and energy and *power*.

They shine naturally, spontaneously, just like the sun.

When I ask kids the question about singing they all, unreservedly, jump up and down, raise their hands and say, "Yes, yes, me ... I want to sing!" Their minds have not yet been impaired by fear.

On one level this book is about returning you gradually and increasingly toward Original Self-Esteem. Helping you to discover that you can experience your own magnificence outside of approval and success, independent of what is happening to you externally.

WHO AM I?

Every day we have thousands and thousands of thoughts and feelings and we think that our thoughts and feelings are our identity. We say: "**I** like this, **I** am happy, **I** am sad, **I** am anxious, **I** am guilty, **I** want this, **I** don't want that, **I** think this or that..."

The 'I' – the identity – is attached to a thought and feeling. And this goes on every day, day after day year after year, for a lifetime. How is it possible for our *true* identity to change hundreds of times a day?

The sense of Self-Esteem that we experience as a child, though not all of the time Original – children also get locked into their thoughts and feelings – is who we really are before the "I" is located in the thought or feeling. When we are naturally expressing and living from the love and inspiration and joy and power, that is our Original Self-Esteem.

This "I" is our infinite and essentially undefinable Spirit, our essence, Pure Consciousness.

When I had this realisation that we are Original Self-Esteem, there was a wonderful sense of calm and peace and joy inside of me.

And that is the point.

If your Self-Esteem is attached to an idea, there is always, at some point, going to be a problem. For instance, if you say, "I don't like his value system, his materialism", for example, your identity is affronted by something that opposes you, this "I".

And so you are proud of your anti-materialist stance,. That is where your identity is located and as soon as someone attacks this identity, your potential to go into fear and anger and lose your balance, lose your love for yourself, lose your power, is increased.

When identity is located in Original Self-Esteem it is solid and stable and flowing and energised and inspired and beautiful. It has a richness and an aliveness that is a joy to be and to live.

We get our sense of identity in terms of Acquired Self-Esteem from other people. They tell us that we are clever or beautiful or kind and soon afterwards what follows is stupid, ugly and cruel. And so we become victims, vulnerable to whatever the world suggests that we are.

WHAT MAKES THE WORLD GO AROUND?

Many years ago I met a yogi named Ian Brebner who said: "It isn't money that makes the world go around, it's fear." I just loved what he said and I will share with you a number of adaptations of this quote throughout this book. When we are in Acquired Self-Esteem, there lurks a fear beneath it – usually unconscious – waiting to be triggered by criticism and rejection.

To feel good only when you are not in a place of fear of what will come at you from the outside is to live in pain.

ORIGINS

My first degree was a Bachelor of Commerce. My parents pushed me into it. I invited them to do the pushing because I was disempowered. I was utterly and devastatingly miserable at this time in my life. I had no interest in economics or accounting and struggled to understand the simple difference between a debit and credit.

I was so miserable in my second year that I kept a depression graph, a score of how much I wanted to die. I never told anyone about it.

I was intensely desperate and equally, desperately private. I was almost entirely powerless as a human being.

When I completed the degree, I was still disempowered and my parents frog-marched me off to a friend of theirs who owned a margarine factory, where I was given the majestic position of personnel officer – a watered down equivalent of today's HR function.

I always jokingly reflect on my time there, saying that I only learned one thing: "eat butter!" This was because of what they do to the sunflower seeds – all the chemicals they add to them – in order to make them palatable.

I left the margarine company and went overseas on my own, travelling around Europe in the middle of winter with some wonderful moments but essentially experiencing a deepening of the depression, including very real thoughts of suicide that had been lurking for so many years.

Living in a communal home in Muswell Hill in London, I one day had the inspired thought: "Maybe becoming a psychologist is it!?"

This option came out of my wanting to heal my own misery and to really try and understand the causes of my own suffering and to help heal the suffering of others.

This was the beginning of experiencing greater fulfilment in my life. I was starting to do what I wanted to do and I felt inspired. This work was a reflection of me, and whenever we do something that is a reflection of who we really are, we are loving ourselves and we are energised and empowered.

This was the first really big expression of my authentic nature in my life.

And there my journey into self-love and power began.

If you are a parent reading this, you might really want to help guide your children toward their inspiration as opposed to pushing them toward the values that *you* hold dear.

Not easy.

Everybody is trying to control everybody else and parenting is one of the places that we do this the most!

Becoming a clinical psychologist was the start of the reconnection with my Original Self-Esteem.

My Original Self-Esteem was experienced in the moments when the work was a spontaneous expression of my magnificence, those beautiful moments of natural, intuitive power and love.

This happens to everyone who has moments
or times when they love what they do!

Interestingly, it was through my lack of work, 30 years later, that this Self-Esteem model emerged and it is linked to my health.

CHRONIC FATIGUE SYNDROME

I have wrestled with a chronic fatigue problem for decades and after consulting the amazing Dr Bruce Hoffman in Calgary, Canada some years ago, I finally got a really accurate diagnosis of the problem. It's very complex and I won't bore you with the details here, save to say that it involves a whole bunch of genetic predispositions, just one of which I would like to mention because it is so little-known.

I have the HLA-DR genotype for mould, essentially meaning I do not produce antibodies to mould which is found in indoor areas that remain damp for 48 hours or more. The mould produces a biotoxin which, for 25% of the population, is deadly.

For a time after the diagnosis, while trying all sorts of new treatments, my energy completely collapsed and with it my clientèle disappeared and my earnings too. I was sitting around one day feeling really deflated, imagining the work pouring in, feeling healthy and busy and rich and then I thought:

"Why do I have to wait for the work to come in for me to start feeling good? After all, that's the victim position. Perhaps I can just imagine feeling as good now as I would feel if I was inundated with clients and money."

It was a turning point in my life and work. From there the model that I'm going to share with you just simply grew on its own; it just came through me and out of me and into my life and it transformed my life and then I began to work with clients, with equally gratifying results.

LOW BLOOD PRESSURE

One of the problems that I had struggled with in the chronic fatigue was low blood pressure, which I had suffered from for at least 30 years and perhaps, unidentified, for longer.

I tried various medications but didn't enjoy the side-effects and certainly alternative remedies such as liquorice root and liquorice tea didn't help at all. Then one day, shortly after creating the second technique in the model *"From pain to love and power 1.0"* I had the inspired thought: "Why don't I measure my blood pressure and then do the Self-Esteem work around the list of pain from the past and see what happens?"

To my astonishment my systolic score (that's the first number in a blood-pressure reading) went up 12 points, from 92 to 104. So I started to do this on a regular basis. In the next month I took 24 readings and my systolic blood pressure went up an average 15 points for each reading!

Only two of the readings did not show an improvement and in both instances I did less than 10 minutes of Self-Esteem work prior to taking the second reading.

Where previously my blood pressure was around 95/60, it was now sitting in the range of 110/70. You can imagine that such a significant increase really knocked me out and energised me significantly in terms of my commitment to doing the work personally and sharing it with my clients.

SUCCESSFUL PEOPLE DON'T HAVE PERFECT SELF-ESTEEM

The second progenitor of this work was an observation I had been making for many years. I had worked with, met and heard interviews with many successful and wealthy people. People who apparently had fantastic Self-Esteem. In many arenas they appeared confident, powerful and commanding.

Yet if one asked the right kinds of questions or if one was privileged, as I was, to have these people talk to me honestly about their difficulties and struggles, what I saw was that, despite areas of great Self-Esteem, there were many areas where these people struggled immensely. They struggled with poor Self-Esteem as much as people who had achieved very little.

The difference was that their success supported and masked the areas of negativity and so these negative areas were not really noticed or talked about much by other people.

In addition, I have often asked my coaching clients who have had issues with their Self-Esteem the following question: "Think about the most skillful leader you have encountered in all of your business experience. Have you seen them anxious, doubtful and uncertain at times?" And of course they would say: "Yes."

I would then ask: "Can you see that in these moments their Self-Esteem has probably dipped and that this is what you saw *publicly!* If you had access to their private negative thoughts and feelings in those moments, what would you see?"

My clients would, of course, smile knowingly.

What I realised is that the reason for negative Self-Esteem running so deeply inside of, or beside such confidence, was that much of the positive Self-Esteem was Acquired.

It was acquired by affirmation and success, and these two qualities are immensely temporary.

> *This work is a movement away from the success-approval model to the "I am lovable as I am" model.*

You might argue that affirmation is always followed by criticism in a continuous cycle, but that success isn't, that often successful people remain so for decades.

The problem is how you define it.

You might be number one in your field, but if you are a sportsman you're not going to win every major tournament or every world championship gold medal, and if you're in business then you are going to have bad months or bad years, even if the general trend is upwards.

And what I find with very successful people is that they are often immensely perfectionistic and even though their business might be doing unbelievably well, making a profit of $500 million a year, if the next year begins badly and if profits are down just 2% or 3%, the anxiety sets in and the negativity and doubt and poor Self-Esteem rears its head.

The answer to this issue, is this book!

The focus is on building Self-Esteem irrespective of external validation or success.

That is a place of true love and power

This is not to say that one shouldn't achieve and acquire "things".

The problem is that in our culture this "acquisition" is the goal. It needs to be a by-product, an extra, an add-on.

What I also find is that our enjoyment and satisfaction of the external things – the house, the car, the beautiful partner, the kids – *is greater when we have the Esteem, before we acquire them!*

WHAT IS GENUINE SELF-ESTEEM?

Our culture teaches us a lie. A myth, which has been believed since ... forever.

It teaches us that the primary way to feel good is to have good things happen to us.

We think that we need approval and success and that things should go "our way" and then all will be well. In the last few decades it has also taught us that to live inspired and to follow your dream is a really good thing, but unfortunately the approval-success model is still overwhelmingly in control of most people most of the time.

As long as we believe that success and approval are the source of our good Self-Esteem, we are Victims of external circumstance. A Victim is someone who is controlled by the world, who feels good or bad because the world dictates so, because good things happen or bad things happen.

It doesn't matter whether it is good or bad, this "happening". The point is that we are like puppets, simply being played by external circumstances.

There is a terrible, inexorable irony here. The more we resist and dislike the "bad" things that happen to us, the more disempowered we become, and the more disempowered we become, the worse the resistance gets. So we fall deeper and deeper into this pit of Victimhood, resisting the very fabric of life. And all of this, based on a fantasy that what is happening right now, *shouldn't be happening*!

I mentioned that fear makes the world go around. Well I believe that fear is created by the need for control, the need to control events in the future and indeed we try to change and control the past, in our heads!

What's really important to understand is that resistance and control are Siamese twins: inseparable. Resistance is disliking something you or someone else does and control is wanting to turn you or someone else into something different.

TRIPARTITE MONSTERS

And so fear, resistance and control are the tripartite monsters that keep us in a place of disempowerment and suffering.

To go beyond this self-destructive and illusory position is a relief of immense proportions. It is power, it is freedom, it is liberation and it is Mastery.

It is transformation at the highest level and this is what this book, this method is about.

The chameleon changes in response to the colour of its environment. For most people, most of the time, we are emotional chameleons. Our emotional state is almost entirely dictated to by the outside world and by the degree of resistance we have to external circumstance. To come into true emotional and spiritual Mastery is to discover that there is something beyond this.

Being a Victim makes us immensely vulnerable. It makes us so vulnerable that it is – to adapt Alan Paton's great phrase – beyond the describing of it.

We are so immersed in this vulnerability to external events, so dependent on what happens externally, that we rarely see, at the deepest of levels, what we are doing.

And even if we do have moments when we do see what is happening, the moments are so overshadowed by the inexorable and ubiquitous sense that the only way to feel good is to have something good happen to us, we remain essentially blind as to how we are victims and to the possibility that we can transform this.

Acquired Self-Esteem comes after Original Self-Esteem. It is learned and, because it is learned, it can be unlearned.

What is really very fascinating is that everybody has some experience of Original Self-Esteem, but we do not get the significance, or ascribe the true meaning to what is happening when we are in this state.

In other words, few people notice Original Self-Esteem for what it is and when it is happening.

FLOW STATES

I have asked dozens of clients what meaning they ascribe to the following type of experience:

They are about to give an important presentation. They are anxious and negatively self-conscious, worried about failure and rejection. The presentation starts and they are absorbed in their own psychology and concern for their own well-being. At this point it is not going well. They are tense and the room is tense.

Then suddenly there is a click, an inexplicable switch into flow and authenticity and spontaneity. People commonly call this the "zone" or a "flow" state.

All thoughts of how they are doing and being perceived dissolve and it is as if the presentation is just doing itself.

And it is!

Original Self-Esteem is where the authentic Pure Consciousness that we are does the "doing"! There is no personality or identity or individual that is doing this; it is simply the movement of pure energy, pure Spirit, actively unselfconscious.

Our greatest Self-Esteem happens when the self disappears!

And here's the thing. When people have this experience, they say: "That was amazing", or "That was wonderful", or "I was fantastic".

But they're missing the point!

What actually happened was that their conditioned, secondary psyche, their Acquired Self-Esteem, dissolved. Pure Consciousness, their Spirit, was moving them. Their personality got out of the way.

It was displaced by the true, natural, original energy that they are.

To put it another way, their self-consciousness dissolved. Many of the techniques in this book are really about dissolving the self-consciousness, which puts you into Acquired Self-Esteem.

This kind of experience usually happens by accident. This work will enable this kind of experience to happen more and more often by *design*, as a result of doing the exercises, practicing the techniques!

It is Original Self-Esteem by design!

It will no longer be an accident for you. It will become a by-product of your dissolving the fears and anxieties and fantasies which reflect the nature of Acquired Self-Esteem.

Many people have had the experience of being criticised or attacked and being untouched by it. As though the external attack has nothing to do with us and has no power to reach our vulnerability and hurt. Yet these experiences happen by accident and so we do not see that they can become a way of being. A way of life that we can create, rather than appearing as an accident, a moment of chance never to happen again, until the next moment of chanc`e occurs.

I spent decades of my life desperately trying to get out of the Victim position, succeeding some of the time but, essentially, failing. I had many, many moments where I clicked into the flow state or the zone, but was, generally speaking, controlled by the anxiety and Acquired Self-Esteem of the Victim position.

This work completely turned me around, which isn't to say I never feel like a Victim. But the intensity and duration of these moments has been vastly reduced, which inspired me to start working with my clients.

METABOLISING EXPERIENCE

Acquired Self-Esteem is what our culture drives. We want to become a "somebody" who leaves a legacy, who creates wealth, who is esteemed in everyone else's eyes, who acquires possessions and who supposedly feels "secure" in this.

Nothing wrong with that, but no matter how great your legacy, or how much wealth you create, or how safe and secure you try to feel, you will still feel somehow incomplete, unsafe, vulnerable, because you are essentially standing outside of your power.

Real power is vital, curious, creative, energised, loose, open, loving, joyful and *a-causal!* Real power is your true nature, before anything happens to you and...

It can digest any experience.

You know the way we say: "I cannot stomach him, or *that* behaviour or *that* situation?"

We are saying that some person is so intolerable, or what they did is so intolerable that we cannot accept what they are, we have to reject them and *we can't digest it!* Anything you reject and which you can't digest puts you in the Victim position, and your power potentially dissolves.

MY RESEARCH

I worked with the beautiful Sedona Method for many years. One of the major components of this model is the idea that we are run through with the need to be in control. I was so obsessed with this idea that one day I decided to do some research. I decided to check out how many times in a day I had a desire to control, or resist, some event.

So I put some wheat-free bread in the toaster. I burnt it (immediate resistance to the black toast). Then I wanted to throw it in the dustbin – guilt ..."don't waste food" (another resistance), then the rebellious thought: "I don't want to eat black toast" (next resistance). Into the bin it went (with some guilt – another resistance!). Now I'm waiting for the next piece of toast to be done. I'm getting hypoglycaemic and irritable (another resistance). That's five resistances in about two minutes.

Seven hours later I had counted 257 resistances and I missed at least half of them because I wasn't fully awake to the reality of what was happening!

My estimate is that the average person has 500 to 1 000 resistances a day, depending on the pressures they face on that particular day.

Now you may be thinking that I am exaggerating. Many people doubt me, so let me illustrate further. You wake up in the morning and these are your thoughts:

"I don't want to get up, I'm tired, I hate Mondays, I hate the showering and brushing teeth and getting the kids organised, I wish my husband would stop complaining (and that's not just one thought, because as he starts complaining there are remembered, repeated resistances to him every time he has opened his mouth and there are internal dialogues around how long he's been complaining and will he ever stop and should I confront him about it again ... yes I will ... no I won't ... yes I will) and I'm anxious about the presentation to the client this morning, and if we don't get the deal then the overdraft is going to be a problem and then I'm going to fight with my husband more..."

That's about 10 resistances (excluding all of the ruminations about the husband's complaining) and about 20 thoughts (again excluding the ruminations about the husband) in the space of 10 seconds *and you're not even out bed yet!*

It's been estimated that we have 30 000 to 50 000 thoughts a day. But by now I hope that you're getting that it's probably a conservative estimate. If you have one a second, that's 3 600 per hour, which is 36 000 in 10 hours!

Please note that in the above dialogue at least half of the thoughts are resistances. And so what I'm illustrating here is the magnitude, the degree to which we do resistance.

Please note, these numbers are in a sense misleading. Why? Because you might wake up with anxious thoughts about money and they sit with you for most of the day ... week ... month ... your life! So is that one thought or is it the same thought repeated 30 times a day?

I don't think it matters. The point is we are deeply, deeply embedded in the Victim position in relation to most of life. Yes, there are times when we are optimistic and positive and confident and yet even within these times we are very often having resistances and anxieties.

And the bottom line is that this ruminative thinking reflects a lack of self-love and a loss of power.

SECOND-ORDER RUMINATIVE THINKING

I had a really fascinating experience recently. I noticed that very often when I had a ruminative thought, such as "I don't want to get up", what would follow would be a judgement and an attempt to change that thought, such as "Just relax, you don't have an option", or "It's only another two days of work this week and then it's the weekend", or "Stop resisting reality."

So in the italicised paragraph above you could add in another whole ream of thoughts which are judgements about the primary thoughts.

I call this second-order ruminative thinking. And so in the above paragraph where I mentioned that we have 10 resistances before we're even out of bed, you can probably add on another 10 resistances in the "second-order" category!!!

It's mind boggling.

It's incessant.

And it drives us crazy.

Later on I will share a magnificent meditative technique to deal with this second-order level of judgement.

THE STRUCTURE OF THIS BOOK

This book is a series of techniques and practices designed to help you to move into Original Self-Esteem, into original love and power. It is essentially a mix of the theory behind the practices and the techniques themselves.

I have separated the theory and the techniques for easier reading and to give you faster and easier access to the techniques. It's easier when they are grouped together in one section. Part 1 is the theory and Part 2 covers the techniques.

You might want to read one piece of the theory and then work with each technique after that, or read all of the theory and then go to the techniques after that.

Do it in your own, Original way. We're all different, and our personalities need to learn new things in different ways. So trust your own instincts and preferences – after all, they're a part of your original nature.

Interestingly, this model was *not* created as a theory. The practical exercises always came first and then the theory evolved out of that. Not surprising, as my primary interest is in creating methods and models that transform Self-Esteem, not in creating theories to do this, as interesting as the theories might be.

NO LOVE, NO POWER

I want to conclude my introduction by sharing with you some of the ways in which we don't love ourselves, some of the ways in which we disempower ourselves.

These are the issues that we will work on in this book:

- I have to be perfect, I can't make mistakes.

This need for perfection is expressed in multitudes of ways: don't see the hole in my sock, or my cracked tooth, or my messy house, or my irritation or anger, or my mistakes, or my selfishness, or my manipulativeness. Or simply: "I mustn't fail on this project, in this job, as a parent or as a partner," or "I am bad if I have failed".

Every time we have these thoughts and the feelings that accompany them we are doing the opposite of loving ourselves. We are in deep judgement of ourselves and our power dissolves. Which leads to...

- Letting people bully us, manipulate us, control us. This is giving our power away to them and not loving ourselves enough to take care of ourselves.

- Endlessly seeking and trying to manoeuvre the world and ourselves in order to create harmony. Presenting a false sense of goodness or kindness to the world, which isn't what we really feel, what we really are, but which makes us acceptable. We dilute our authenticity.

We do this by smiling on the outside when we're not smiling on the inside. By hypervigilantly looking out for those criticising us and trying to calm them down and pacify them. This is exhausting and, most importantly, *it is being brutally unkind to ourselves.*

Leo Buschalia – he was often called Dr Love – was a professor of Special Education at the University of California. He tells a story of how a peach can only be a peach; it can't be a banana or an orange. You can only be what you are. If you are banana trying to be some other kind of fruit, you will end up being a fruit salad!

And when we are not being our authentic selves, that's what we feel like – a crazy fruit salad.

And so a deeply profound aspect of this work is to find the joy, the love dancing within.

- When we do all of the above you might have noticed that what you are doing is endlessly *justifying* yourself to the world. You do this in your behaviour and you do this in your thinking. You leave the situation and you say to yourself, "Well, I needed to speak honestly there, because the person was being unkind to me", and then you get into this long dialogue back and forth, trying to justify why you are honest.

If you loved yourself completely, there would be no need to justify yourself in any way – with no one to blame and no ruminations.

- Allowing fear to control us. Everyone gets frightened: it is part of the human condition. This trait helps us to establish when there is danger and to know when to fight or to flee. However, fear takes over psychologically, it is overdetermined. This work will help you to dissolve your fears so that you can stand in love and stand in power and go for what you want and express your nature in its unique way, which really just wants to shine in the world, unadulterated and energised and joyful, just like a child.

Where there is no second-guessing of yourself, no checking to see if something will work or fail or if you will be approved of or not. To dissolve your fears and to come into love and power is to return to Original Self-Esteem.

- When your to-do list and the kids and your work are overwhelming, the love and the power has leaked out of you. That is what stress is: "I can't cope, it's all too much for me. I want to run and hide and escape to a Greek island", or simply, "I want to die".

Love and power can hold all of the stresses and strains and pains of life. This work is designed to lead you into that space where this holding can begin to happen.

- The belief that you must succeed in the ways in which society dictates. You must be thinner and stronger and more attractive and more extrovert and you must make a lot of money and love your work and be successful in marriage and have a beautiful home and not have anxiety and experience hurt and pain.

This is a monumentally tall order. The order is so tall that even extremely successful people by most standards do not feel the fulfilment that they would expect their success to afford them.

In addition, nothing wrong with acquiring the home, the kids, the BMW etc, but this book will help you to dissolve your belief that these things will ultimately fulfil you at a really deep level. They are beautiful gifts, but they are not your essence, the true shining light that you are.

- We have a tendency to fixate on getting happiness externally, on "getting". So, in this work we find ways to get gratification and happiness on the inside. It's an internal, energetic thing. To find it internally is far more rewarding.

• Learning to love yourself for no reason.

This is our greatest blessing. Experiencing love a-causally – without a cause, when nothing is happening and most especially when we are being rejected or when we have failed. To stand in this place and to know the true love of self is a gift beyond my ability to describe.

WHY DID I CREATE THIS WORK?

I must first thank a dear friend of mine Desiree Marie-Leedo. She does amazing work around moving on after divorce or a breakup and living the life you love. I was discussing this new idea around Self-Esteem that was just evolving and she suggested I create a video course around it. http://bit.ly/videotrainingse

I did and the book soon followed.

The original idea arose as a result of an incredibly strong need to feel better about myself, more engaged with the world and energised about life, rather than resistant to life, on the back foot, feeling that life was too difficult, too stressful for me, filled with anxiety. I had spent my life looking for love externally and I just knew it didn't work.

This enabled me to feel more energised, vital, spirited and engaged with life.

When I discovered how well it worked, I was unstoppable in sharing it with my clients.

I hope you enjoy it as much as I and they have.

PART ONE
The Theory

CHAPTER 1

What is Love and Internal Power?
Why Are They so Important?

To love yourself … is freedom!
The belief that we should be loved … cripples us!
Don't limit the degree to which you love yourself,
by believing that you've reached your limit!

I see 'him' in my thoughts
I'm threatened
My body contracts
Power has leaked out of my system.
I gave it all to 'him.'

I hate the feeling and slowly, privately
I concoct a story for the world
That tells you all how awful 'he' is,
A long and convoluted story,
So elaborate, so convincing.
The truth concealed
I run from 'him' because I have no power.
What a lie to live with for this long life.

Mark Peter Kahn.

Self-love is the foundation of Self-Esteem and internal power is its partner.

If someone criticises you and you believe them, you are not loving yourself and you have no power. Their opinion of you has overwhelmed your opinion of yourself.

If you criticise yourself, you collapse your power.

If you fail to achieve a particular goal you've been aiming at and you perceive that that failure is something negative or bad about you, that judgement destroys your power.

If you are working on a new project, or trying to work with a new piece of software that you don't understand, or you are listening to someone whom you think is smarter than you and you can't understand them *and you feel inadequate or incompetent,* then you have given away your power and you are not loving yourself.

If you avoid difficult conversations, conflicts and negotiations, you have lost your power.

LEVELS WE DON'T NOTICE

When you are anxious about being late, or early for an appointment, there is no love inside of you.

If someone is boring you and you have a resistance to the boredom – which most people do – then there is no love inside of you.

If someone is irritating you, reflecting traits you don't like, there is no love inside of you.

When you're feeling really good or you think you are feeling good and then any of the above happens and you suddenly feel very uncomfortable, then there is no love inside of you.

If someone contradicts a value that is of importance to you, e.g. they say that slavery was a good thing and you feel very uncomfortable, then there was no love inside of you in that moment.

You're really excited about some achievement at work and your intimate partner is unenthusiastic about it, or just ignores your excitement, there was no love there. We crave excitement in our culture, but excitement is *not* love!

Mostly we are very needy of the approval of those close to us.

And when they don't give it, we do not see that this is a deficit of love inside of **us!**

You can see that what I'm saying is that very few people are truly immersed in love much of the time.

How do I know all of this? Because I tested it on myself and I realised that when I could fill myself with love, none of these issues was a problem. So when people tell you that they're fine, that everything is okay and they are feeling really good, actually this usually isn't entirely true.

The feeling good is a veneer that covers up a great deal of lack of self-love.

When you're filled with love, nothing and
nobody is going be a problem for you.

You remember those thousand resistances a day that I mentioned in the introduction? Well, every moment of resistance is a loss of love. Fill yourself with love and there is no resistance. Fill yourself with love and you begin to open yourself into an appreciation of life that never existed before.

For me this is truly a miracle.

We are trained to look for love on the outside. So when we are feeling good, we are actually usually hypervigilant externally for what is going to continue to make us feel good and what might make us feel bad. So you go off to a social function, you are watching a sporting event with friends or are just having a cup of tea or dinner with them and all is going well until somebody says something that you find insulting or rude or antisocial, it can upset your entire evening.

Which means that the good feelings you had, the love that you felt before this incident was brittle and fragile. When you realise this, what you can do is really truly begin to love yourself so that none of these external problems begin to matter very much.

Personally, I have found this the most incredible blessing in my life and I still have some way still to go.

EXPECTATIONS

It isn't money that makes the world go around;
it's our expectations and fantasies.

We have endless fantasies and expectations about how life should be.

It's the weekend, which means I *should* be able to relax and have a good time. I'm going on holiday and I *should* have a wonderful, beautiful, uplifting and relaxing time.

I'm coming home from work and I've had a good day and I expect my partner to be relaxed and comfortable and happy.

I put in an offer on a beautiful home – it's my *dream* home – and I'm desperate for the offer to come through.

I'm desperate to get a new job to start a new career and I have endless fantasies about how wonderful it's going to be.

Certainly all of these things can be wonderful, but most of the time there is a let-down. Things don't work out as well as we had hoped or as well as we had fantasised.

And the bottom line is that we're having these fantasies only because there's not enough love right here right now without anything having to be different. So the solution is simply to learn to fill yourself with love right here right now and then nothing needs to change in order for you to feel better.

Why is it difficult to love ourselves? Because our conditioning is so focused on us being kind to others and loving others that to love ourselves is, for most people, foreign and difficult. We have little or no reference point for doing this.

WHAT IS POWER?

Power is energy and energy is life.

No power, no life.

Power is Spirit. When we are filled with Spirit, we are filled with energy and vitality. We move *toward* life with anticipation, aliveness and a sparkle in our eyes. We are enlivened with Spirit.

So much of the time, when we feel that life is too much, we are moving *away* from life.

We are in *avoidance*.

Avoidance will kill your Spirit, your power.

A person who is alive and powerful, generates thought, movement, creativity and action. They are not easily pushed over, disempowered. They do not believe judgements from others *or from themselves*.

We often have powerful thoughts, but if they do not get translated into movement (action), we stagnate, we become passive and frozen in "inactive thought". Disempowered people are usually not good at *action!* They are stuck in thought.

And so *power is movement.*

"Life cannot be lived in the head."

When we are depressed we have little energy and little power. Without power there is no movement and no life. When we're inspired, we are filled with energy. It is an energy that comes from deep within us and it creates thought and propels us into action. Creative power is unstoppable. We don't even have to *decide* to do something; it just seems to do *itself.* There is doing without a "doer".

And so, the deepest level of power is consciousness, the energy that is contained in all things.

Clarity is power.

Energetically, if you are clear intellectually and you can translate this into words and action, then your power is centred in the solar plexus while the mind is clear.

It is really fascinating for me how people lose this clarity.

A woman is struggling with her husband. He is aggressive, controlling, disrespectful and hostile much of the time. When he behaves like this she wants to dump him, leave and get rid of him.

Then when he is not behaving in this way, he is reasonable, and kind and decent.

When he behaves like this she sees him as a good person and a good husband and someone whom she wants to stay with.

The problem is she flip-flops from outraged and indignant and inferior to forgiving and accepting of him. There is no clarity in her mind because she cannot see the big picture.

A vast proportion of people behave this way. Their inability to stand back from the situation and to get the overall *clarity* of what is happening eludes them, and so they have no power. The mind is a Victim of whatever is happening externally. The husband is either terrible or good.

This clarity is wisdom and power. Its acquisition is not much talked about in our culture.

In addition, when we get anxious, the danger is that our energy moves into the head, as we ruminate endlessly about the problem, which results in indecision and uncertainty. Now we are trying to solve a problem from a place that is disempowered – a confused mind.

Many people fear being powerful because it can increase conflict and the chance of hurting others is raised. Their belief systems around these issues – a lack of clarity – prevents them from connecting with their power.

You don't get power for free. It has costs attached to it.

DEGREES OF POWER

There are degrees of power. In the same way as a lightbulb can burn with the energy of 30 watts, 50 watts or 100 watts, so human beings have degrees of power.

Some people have a great deal of physical energy, which is one form of power. So they don't need a lot of sleep and they can do a lot of things because the body is healthy and it generates a lot of energy. But they don't necessarily have psychological power.

They are easily disabled or immobilised by threat or challenge.

Some people have psychological power but little spiritual power. Spiritual power is wisdom – not just thinking it, but applying it. It's about being open-hearted and living without fear and trusting oneself and life. It is acting with spontaneous, non-judgemental, loving courage.

It is loving oneself independent of the external world.

Spiritual power also enables the release of emotions very quickly. It's not holding on to them.

If you feel threatened or anxious or angry when someone disagrees with you, you have probably lost your power. If someone remarks on a character trait of yours and you feel and get defensive, you've lost your power. If you want to avoid conflict, you have lost your power.

Sensitive people struggle particularly with these issues, but even people who aren't sensitive do as well. They often just don't know it.

Most people are desperate about being respected. When we feel disrespected and hurt by it, our power has dissolved and usually our Self-Esteem with it.

EATING FROM THE TREE OF SELF-CONSCIOUSNESS

Genesis got it wrong!

Adam and Eve did not eat the apple from the tree of knowledge of good and evil, they ate from the tree of *self-consciousness*. (I'm obviously joking to make a point here.) This is the ability to stand apart from who we are and to reflect, question, commentate and ruminate about who we are.

Self-consciousness is a blessing and a curse. The blessings are obvious: we think about our lives, we reflect on them, we change direction, we strategise and problem solve, we create, we evolve and we grow.

The curse is that in becoming self-aware we fall into the well of ruminative self-consciousness. We sink into a realm of ghosts and shadows, of doubt and anxiety, of guilt and self-recrimination.

It is a fall from grace into hell and it feels like hell because it is an endless, painful cycle of negative thinking, over which we have little control.

When we are infants we are free of self-consciousness. Wordsworth's beautiful line, "Heaven lies about us in our infancy", so aptly reflects this.

There is a wonderful test that describes this movement into self-consciousness.

It is called the "rouge test." If you put a spot of rouge on the forehead of a child of six months and get the child to look at itself in the mirror, it just looks, innocently, not recognising itself. It has no self-consciousness.

When it gets to about 12 months old it recognises its reflection for the first time. How do we know that this is where self-consciousness begins? Because the child will touch the spot of rouge in a way that it is evident that it is aware that it is touching its own forehead. Before this happens the child appears to look at its reflection as if it is looking at someone else – no *self*-awareness.

Parents get really excited when a child has self-awareness, when it recognises its own name, its separateness from everything. The parents are celebrating the blessings.

The curse is not usually so well recognised.

When we are in ruminative self-consciousness we leave this moment, the power of Now. We split ourselves into two. There is us, watching ... us!

And love, on the inside, dissolves.

"Do they like me, am I going to mess up, I wish I was different, better, thinner, cuter, kinder..." and "They are stupid, or cleverer than me, or richer and more successful than me...", on and on, endlessly judging and rating and scoring ourselves and the world.

I am in great debt to the work of Dr John Demartini for his contribution to my life and work and most particularly for his phrase:

> *"There is a universal law which says that nothing can manifest without two sides."*

This phrase has two basic meanings and many beautiful applications.

On the one hand, it means that every trait or characteristic has an opposite: kind – cruel, happy – sad, creative – destructive, truthful – dishonest, success – failure and so on.

The next level down is that each trait has a benefit and a drawback. So success obviously is very beneficial on multiple levels but it also has deficits in that it leads to complacency, egocentricity, mistakes and a loss of the drive that was there before the success.

The double-sidedness of this process is ironic. We notice ourselves as being clever, attractive, successful, good, kind, contributing to society, giving, being creative, making money, achieving in the myriads of ways our culture admires, but each of these qualities has a downside: stupid, ugly, a failure, bad, cruel and so on.

And so self-consciousness gives birth to the anxiety of criticism and failure and the guilt and shame that follow soon thereafter.

And so, as I am writing this now, I am feeling inspired, which is wonderful, watching new ideas emerge from consciousness, without me having to do anything, just noticing this arising of thoughts and pictures and concepts and images. How beautiful.

On the other hand, there is a subtle contraction in my body, and sense of driving toward the next word, the next idea, a vague anxiety: "Will I get all of these inspirations onto the page? Will I be able to organise them adequately, perfectly?" – a fear that it will not all come together as I want it to, as beautifully as I would like it to.

And so I dissolve these "contractions into the future" in love and power and I return to my original sense of inspiration – and that dissolving is the work of this book.

Emotional and physical contraction is the
self-conscious loss of power!

When we are self-conscious, we have bitten into the apple of self-reflection and pain and we begin to suffer. *This is the wound that begins inside of us at around 12 months old.*

This is the pain that we wrestle with our whole lives. Up to this point we are in Original Self-Esteem, unaware of right and wrong, good and bad. Beyond this point we start to move into Acquired Self-Esteem, feeling good because of success and approval or bad because of failure and rejection.

I am writing this in the bushveld in Botswana, going out on game drives, watching original nature, the animals, totally un-selfconscious. I take photographs of them, they just sit there, aware of me, but *not watching* themselves. I see a lion and a lioness mating.

People cannot do that and be watched unselfconsciously, can they?

People *cannot even let you take photographs of them without stiffening and tightening,* contracting through the self-conscious awareness of self: "What do I look like? What about my nose? My hair is a mess, these clothes are old and ugly..."

I think that's one of the reasons that people these days, when having their picture taken, take on all sorts of weird poses – sticking their tongues out and pouting their lips. It's a defence against the anxiety of just being themselves, *unselfconsciously.*

A new neurosis has even emerged: obsessive attempts at taking the perfect selfie!

How many people do you know can take a compliment utterly and completely unselfconsciously?

You say to someone, "Lovely outfit" and what does their body do? It contracts, they look uncomfortable, because your compliment raises their doubt and pleasure simultaneously.

It is a confused mess of elation and inferiority, a sense of being pumped up and manic, coupled with the fear that they don't deserve the compliment and a mind that is now in overdrive: "Do I really, really look good? Can I trust this person? Are they being honest? Maybe they're just being nice ... they are a bit of a rescuer ... I've noticed that they do this ... a lot ... they're fake, yes, I know they are ... it really drives me nuts about them ... they really piss me off ... I look like crap, I know I do ... this dress is tired and old and old fashioned..."

And out of their mouths comes this weak, passive-aggressive, inauthentic, "Thanks."

They are speaking from the wound of self-consciousness.

A compliment is a gift. To receive it is to be in Original Self-Esteem, in unselfconsciousness. It is to say "Thank you" with an open heart. No internal dialogue, no checking and questioning and doubting and commentating. Just "Thank you". It's simple, it's pure, and uncontaminated with ruminations and stories.

AN ENLIGHTENED LAMA

For many years I wondered if the Dalai Lama was enlightened, a spiritually awakened being and then, one day, I think I got my answer.

I was watching a panel discussion of which he was one of the participants. There were about a thousand people in the audience.

The panelists were being set up with throat mics, and during this process, the Dalai Lama sneezed. His sneeze was broadcast throughout the entire speaker system, very loudly!

The audience burst out laughing. He was focusing on something else and then suddenly realised the big sound of the sneeze that he heard through the speaker system was himself.

Most people would have cringed with embarrassment and apology. The Dalai Lama smiled broadly and then laughed completely innocently at what had happened. In other words, with a complete lack of self-consciousness, a complete lack of apology, embarrassment or shame. A complete lack of needing to cover up his unexpected sneeze.

I think the man is spiritually awake. He has dropped his self-consciousness. Do you want to be like that?

IS STILLNESS RUNNING THE WORKSHOP?

Some years ago I had a personal experience, which reflected this self-consciousness for me in the most extraordinary way.

At the time I was running a series of workshops in organisations around a process I had created, called *Values Conversations*. I got a really big piece of work for a large company where I would be working with eight executive teams sharing my approach.

The first of these divisions I went into was a complete disaster. Over the years I had received remarkably positive feedback around my values work and my facilitation skills generally.

This occasion was not the case. My feedback was a slaughter-house.

I was told I was boring, inappropriate and hadn't done my homework. At first, I took it rather personally, losing all of my power. But then new information came to light, and I realised that I had been caught in the crossfire of the politics between head office and this particular division. The feedback had nothing, or at least very little, to do with me.

Nevertheless, when I went in to do my second workshop the next week, with the next team, I was still very anxious. My disempowerment had returned.

Just before the workshop commenced, I noticed my *negative self-consciousness*, my anxiety, my sense of foreboding and stress and threat at what might transpire, given the disaster of the previous group.

So I said to myself quietly, as the group was taking their seats:

"Is Mark running the workshop or is the Stillness running the workshop?"

What is "the Stillness"?

It is my shorthand for connecting me with power and love.

It shifts me into the *energetic signature* of these qualities, and in this instance it shifted me instantaneously out of this state of *negative self-consciousness* and simply into a "being-ness" a "flow state", where I wasn't thinking about the last failed workshop or how this group was going to perceive me or whether they had heard about the problems in the previous group.

From our 8:30 am start until 10:30 am tea, the workshop was pure, creative joy.

There was an amazing connection. I felt inspired. The group was energised and engaged. We broke for tea and, as I walked out of the room to go to the restroom, I remember saying to myself, metaphorically pumping my fists in the air like a tennis player winning a beautiful cross-court shot to beat an opponent, "Yes!!!"

And what happened after tea? My performance dipped.

Why?

Because I had moved into *positive self-consciousness*. I was just a little bit manic, a little bit high, self-consciously reflecting on how well it had gone and how fabulous I was.

So I went back to the Stillness and my performance improved.

"I don't want to drop my positive self-consciousness."

People are usually happy to drop their *negative self-consciousness* because it is so clearly painful, but many don't want to drop the *positive self-consciousness* because it apparently feels so good. I say apparently, because in the manic excitement there is, hidden beneath it, a sense of pain, the pain that knows this excitement can't last and that it is exaggerated Self-Esteem.

It is usually temporary and lacks substance.

THE BOTTOM LINE

Self-consciousness is a deep wound of powerlessness and it can be healed. The techniques in this method are designed to catalyse this healing into power and love.

TWO DEFINITIONS

I have two definitions of Self-Esteem:

1. Acquired Self-Esteem is having a sense of worth that is *dependent* on and derived from external events.

2. Original Self-Esteem is having a sense of worth that is *independent* of external events.

I recently read an amazing piece of research that supports the idea that there are two definitions.

It was found that 82% of kids aged six years had confidence – Self-Esteem – regarding learning new tasks. This had dropped to 18% at the age of 16.

What happened to that 64% of confidence?

Where did it go?

What destroyed it?

Parenting, culture, education?

These numbers are horrifying, devastating.

Yes, we send kids to school and we teach them things, but the way we teach them and the attitude toward learning and teaching is destructive to our sense of worth much of the time.

> *It is very important to understand that I am not recommending that you become isolated from others. An island that is never open to warmth and love and collaboration and support from other people. In order for children to access and express their Original Self-Esteem they need to be loved in the first place. If they are not loved, they will not be able to manifest and express this Original Self-Esteem.*

FORGIVENESS

Our culture is just a genius at teaching us how to judge things, including ourselves.

Our culture teaches us that we are good when we do the right thing according to the norms of the culture and we are bad if we do the wrong things according to the norms of the culture.

These norms are *relative*. They change from culture to culture and within cultures over time, but tell that to someone punting a cultural value with fundamentalist vehemence!

That 64% loss of confidence between the ages of six and 16 occurs because we believe the judgements the culture gives us.

And the reason we need to forgive ourselves is that we have judged ourselves in the first place.

Actually, if there was no judgement there would be no need for forgiveness.

So the first step is to forgive all of the judgements we have made about ourselves.

Just imagine what it would feel like if you could truly forgive yourself for everything you thought was bad about you … then all of the judgements would dissolve, yes?

If you stopped judging yourself completely, if you simply honoured everything that you were, there would be nothing to forgive. So once you've forgiven yourself, the next step is to no longer judge!

> *"Everybody's doing their best, even when they're not doing their best."*

I realised the truth of this some years ago when I was observing the business dealings of a psychopath. Everyone and everything that came into his realm was an object for his manipulations and for his own selfish ends. He never gave anything except to enhance himself.

And then I realised that this is how he was; this was his personality and had probably been like this since he was three years old. There was nothing he could do about it.

When the rest of us, who aren't psychopaths, behave selfishly, or neurotically, or incompetently, when we are overwhelmed by our anxiety and our performance dips, when we are tired and unmotivated, this is simply what we are and we cannot help it.

And then perhaps we start to make choices that change our lives and that's wonderful, but until that moment before we made that choice, we couldn't do anything else.

Everybody is simply being who they are.

When you realise this, a great peace can arise inside of you, because you can accept the world and everyone else and yourself as just being what they are, and right now it is simply that.

What has just happened has just, well, happened and it can't be changed.

SUCCESS AND SELF-ESTEEM

What is really, really fascinating is that even apparently successful and powerful people can have huge power deficits under pressure and, because they are successful, they encounter pressure often!

Their confidence and power in many areas supports and indeed masks the significance of these losses of power and, in fact, leads us to think they are "normal!" and not often disempowered. And normal – statistically – they are. But what is statistically normal does not have to remain so, and that is one of the important contributions that this book can make to your life.

> *You do not have to think that losses of*
> *power are a normal way of life!*

Or to put it another way: notice the ways in which you lose power that are usually ignored, and *stop giving it away!*

Power is experienced energetically and physically. When we are in our power we are in our body. Western culture is very cerebral. It is a "think therefore I am" culture – with no thanks to René Descartes.

Knowledge and fact acquisition centres us in the head. The mind is very important and so we get to...

THE CONSERVATISM OF CULTURE

Cultures are essentially conservative. It's unavoidable and pernicious.

Mostly we understand the word conservative to have a political meaning, but a much more important understanding is to see conservative as meaning to conserve what has gone before and what exists "now" and to resist anything creative or new that might change this.

Most parents want their children to have the values that they have, to stick to the traditions they adhere to, to dress as they prefer, to use expressions and forms of speech that they like and to follow the customs and rituals that they follow.

Parenting is one of *the* great bastions of conservatism.

When children behave in accordance with their parents' value system, the parents are happy and they believe that they have "good" kids. When the kids rebel, the parents are upset and feel that something is wrong and use every form of manipulation available in order to get the children to behave.

In essence, most parents want their children *not* to be powerful and independent, but to be good, to behave.

Why?

Because it makes the parent's life much easier if they have well behaved children as opposed to wild, creative and re-bellious children. (In the last 20 or so years this has changed to some degree, with parents becoming much more liberal and laissez-faire with their children, which, of course, has its own drawbacks.)

UNIVERSITIES AS BASTIONS OF TRUTH

I studied psychology at university.

Universities are supposed to be bastions of the truth.

They aren't.

Some degree of creativity was encouraged when I was a student, but very often any challenging of an idea that was close to the hearts and minds of my teachers was met with hostility and the kind of authoritarian attitude expressed so perfectly by my parents, who came from another era.

Most people would say that they are in favour of creativity, yet conservatism is the antithesis of creativity.

Most cultures function around their ability to control and manipulate their people with rules and commandments as their weapons.

Our culture prescribes beliefs to control us and we get punished if we behave contrary to these beliefs. Cultures need this control, because if they didn't exercise it, they wouldn't survive.

Any time that someone breaks the rules of the culture they become a threat to the culture, because if enough people break the rules and the rules break down, then all of the cultural norms disappear and something new emerges. This might be a good thing, but cultures seldom see change as good and unless the majority of the population is suffering immensely, as happened, for instance, in the French Revolution.

Great power is to maintain and sustain and enable ourselves as dynamic living fields of energy. This dynamism, when lived, is extraordinarily fulfilling and enriching. It is our birthright. This book is designed to help you to connect with this dynamism.

To conservatism, creativity is death.

In essence, our culture wants to maintain its coherence by getting everybody to conform to the rules of the system. We send our kids to school, but we want them to learn what we have learned. We want them to regurgitate the lessons and teachings and "facts" as we see them. Creativity is espoused but often punished. In the words of Derek Thompson: "American culture worships creativity, but only in the abstract."

This might sound extreme and you might be thinking that I'm exaggerating, but let's take the field of science, which is presumably the most logical and fact-based pursuit of any area of endeavour in our culture.

Many papers and articles and books have been written about the conservatism of science.

Mark Miller says: "We love the concept of creativity and extol the virtues of being creative, but the way we're wired precludes us from fully embracing new ideas."

One would expect scientists to be objective and logical in their thinking and approach to creativity, but this is absolutely not the case.

Let me illustrate:

In the sixth century BC, Pythagoras said that the world was round. Only in the 15th century, when sailors ventured across the globe was it universally accepted that Pythagoras was correct.

In 1543, Copernicus published his findings that the earth was not the centre of the solar system.

It took nearly 200 years before the truth of these findings were accepted by the world.

Charles Darwin withheld his publication of *The Origin of The Species* for eight years, because of his fear of the potential rejection of it.

In 1984, an Australian scientist named Barry Marshall discovered that the bacterium Helicobacter pylori was the cause of most forms of stomach ulcer.

The scientific community laughed at him.

Only in 2005 did he receive the Nobel Prize for his work. It took the scientific community 21 years to acknowledge the validity of this discovery!

Recent research by Kevin Boudreau and his colleagues showed that university faculty experts punished or rejected novel ideas. Experts are highly critical of creative thinking because it challenges their egos. What is really fascinating is that if the ego is challenged, it is because it lacks power!

Acquired Self-Esteem is really a vulnerable ego.

It is only Powerlessness that rejects creativity. It has to reject it because it doesn't feel safe and secure and strong. It is disempowered and many authority figures are fearful of their own lack of Power being exposed.

A research study conducted in 1999 found that teachers who claim to enjoy creative children actually don't enjoy any of the characteristics associated with creativity, such as nonconformity, and obviously this is for the reasons stated above.

I have personally noticed how, when I share new ideas with people, they struggle to accept them and tend to do what is natural in these kinds of instances, which is they refer to what they know in order to try to understand what they don't know. A most amusing paradox, yes?

Some years ago I recommended Dr Demartini's book *The Breakthrough Experience* to a colleague.

She read it and said: "It's lovely to have the things we know confirmed."

Yet there were ideas in this book that I am fairly sure she had had no exposure to, such as love being defined as: "A synthesis and synchronicity of complementary opposites."

What's really interesting in the research that I mention above is that it has been found that "slightly novel" ideas are more likely to be accepted by experts than drastically creative ones. In other words, the expert is saying internally: "Because of my fear and conservatism, I will only accept change in very small degrees."

I believe that this is the same in the general population.

This absolutely concurs with over 30 years of experience that I've had working as a clinical psychologist and 17 years as a management consultant. When I see a client for the first time, I need to be very careful with challenging their perceptions and belief systems. They cannot tolerate something that is too far removed from their belief system. They will usually almost instantaneously reject foreign ideas.

I learned from Dr Demartini that there's no such thing as a broken heart, just a broken fantasy. If I share this immediately, upfront, with a client whose partner of six months or six years has just left them, they'll walk straight out of my office thinking that I'm a nutcase!

I have to build their trust and go slowly and then, when I have their trust, I can begin to share such a perception with them and help them to work with it.

What this means is that if people don't trust me, they are only open to that in me which resonates well for them, which is really about their disempowerment. In other words, they cannot hear something logically and objectively because they are disempowered by their lack of trust of me. They are not able to use their intellect in an objective way to assess whether what I'm saying makes sense or not.

They are disabled by their intellect and emotions!

Scepticism exists because it's useful. If we didn't have the trait of scepticism, we would be incredibly gullible and open to being defrauded and deluded by all sorts of tricksters and charlatans. But it is a continuum.

On the one side we have gullibility and on the other sceptical conservatism. Neither is necessarily a position of Power.

In the middle is power and this power is discernment.

It is the ability to be open and to listen and to question without fear. Very few people live in this space, much of the time.

Regarding my chronic fatigue problem, Dr Hoffman, whom I consulted in Calgary, practises what is called integrative medicine. He uses what is best and what works best from alternative or complementary medicine and what is useful from allopathic medicine.

Most of the specialists in allopathic medicine whom I've consulted over the years tend to have extremely rigid opinions and viewpoints around what they understand to be expert medical opinion.

Interestingly, the "alternative experts" often tend to be fairly rigid in their attachment to their paradigm too!

When I have mentioned to the allopathic practitioners that I have the HLA-DR genotype for mould, a significant cause of my fatigue, they look either bemused, or critical, or disinterested, and mostly just move on with what they are doing, sticking *conservatively* to their paradigm. *They are disempowered by their conservatism and rigidity.*

POWER IN INTERACTION

We tend to be addicted to our values and principles and beliefs, and our identity is attached to them. So people believe in respect or kindness or taking care of the planet or animals, and when these beliefs are challenged, most people get angry, affronted, hurt and indignant.

If you ask most people if they are in control of what they say and do, they will probably say yes.

I don't think so.

Let me illustrate. I was running one of my management development workshops a few years ago and asked for a volunteer from the group to discuss with me some idea or concept that they were very passionate about.

A young man of about 30 years old volunteered. He started to talk about Manchester United, a soccer team that he loved. I recorded the discussion we had. My primary objective was to illustrate the skill of using *Strategic Questions* to dissolve conflict. (See Part 2 of this book).

The young man started to talk passionately about Manchester United. I would then purposely disagree with something he said and then, at times, I would agree with him, or simply ask questions rather than taking a position against him. What's really interesting is that after listening to this interview two or three times I noticed that he was completely and utterly in the Victim position in relation to what I did.

He thought he was in control of himself but every time I opposed him, his tone of voice would go up, he would speak faster and he would get irritated and angry. (He would get *hot & fast & tight* – the Victim position.) When I softened and slowed down and asked questions, he would soften and slow down. (He would get *cool & slow & loose*. The Mastery position.)

The point is that most people are exactly like him. As soon as someone out there says or does something which opposes our strongly held values, we cannot help ourselves but get irritated or upset. This is a loss of power that isn't often recognised.

We give away our Power to someone who disagrees with us.

Isn't it fascinating how power works on an interactive level?

We are so essentially and deeply conservative. We are wanting to control others with our opinions about how things should be, and any change or creative idea that departs from our conservative beliefs is seen as a threat, as a negative.

Disempowerment is really interesting in this regard. It comes in two forms. The passive retreating type and the aggressive overpowering type. The latter is not usually seen as being a problem with power but it is, because internally the "over-powerer" is anxious, threatened and deeply distressed and their *strategy* for dealing with this pain and suffering is to use aggression and bully-boy tactics to manage and mask their internal pain.

Under pressure, the world is, largely speaking, filled with people being "underpowered" and "overpowered". One of the reasons that the world and our institutions appear to be in such desperate shape is that mostly a very big ego is required in order to manage a position of power, because of the way our culture is structured, So the "egos" that get what they want by overpowering other people, are very often in leadership positions, both politically and in business.

And that's just the way it is.

If more people were able to truly come into their power psychologically, we would have less of a problem with our political and business leaders, as well as with the planet as a whole.

ADAPTABILITY AS A FUNCTION OF POWER

The more skilfully and quickly and creatively you can adapt to new situations, the greater your power. Adapt or die: that's the name of the game. But the question is: how *well* you can adapt and how quickly and effectively you can adapt?

What I learned from Gestalt psychology is that people have different ways of adapting.

You encounter something new. Do you go into shock, or threat and reject something completely, or do you assimilate what is workable for you into what you already are? To put it another way, how well do you assimilate what is good for you and how quickly do you spit out what isn't good for you?

In the chapter on *Cultivating Wisdom,* I will be discussing conditioning in some depth. Conditioning is the absorption of values and principles and beliefs given to us by our culture. Most kids take in conditioned beliefs without questioning them and many adults reject that which is original and new.

So we move from being too gullible to being too sceptical.

This is being an unconscious victim.

This is not power. So, your skill and capacity to assimilate effectively is critical if you want to have power. Adaptability is fluid and flexible. Preconceived notions are rigid and brittle. If you meet the world with rigid conservatism, you stagnate.

If you are open and fluid, you can grow.

It is a polarity.

On the one hand we have stagnation, and on the other, growth. Your ability to grow is determined by the degree to which you *want* to grow.

People who are open are powerful. Conservatism is closed and either underpowered or overpowering.

Of all the qualities that I see in clients who come to me for psychotherapy, the most important one is their desire to grow.

The kind of client who wants to come in and sit down and just tell their story every week usually doesn't want to grow much. They don't want to listen, they don't want to take in and learn and adapt. They just want to release their story and then leave. They are addicted to the telling of their stories.

Most people aren't in relationship with each other;
they're in a relationship with each other's stories.

For many people, their pain is so overwhelming and there is so much of it blocked in their unconscious, that all they can do is tell their stories. To not do so would derail them completely. That's just the way it is.

The constellation of pain and hurt and abuse in their lives has made it impossible for them to open themselves up to change, to new ways of being. All they can do is tell their story in order to get temporary relief. They cannot help doing this. They are not trying to do this consciously. They have no choice in the matter.

Oftentimes, people go through a period of needing to just tell their stories and then they start to go deeper and that is when the real healing begins.

The fact that we relate to each other through our stories is one of the reason why only 4% of intimate relationships work. In other words, people are really just relating through a commentary that is removed from their direct emotional experience.

ADDICTIONS AND POWER

Any addiction is a loss of power. Most people associate addiction with alcohol, drugs, cigarettes, chocolates. This is a very, very narrow view.

Just about everybody has some form of addiction. In addition to the traditional addictions, we are addicted to talking *and* to being listened to, to our cellphones, to checking email, to being affirmed by others, to *doing* things, to being approved of, respected, valued, to having harmony and pleasure, to *getting what we want,* to judging and rating everything we see, feel and hear.

These addictions are uncontrolled repetitive behaviours which are not entirely necessary for our survival or in service of efficient, loving and powerful living.

Addictions are an avoidance.

If you are desperate and addicted to having someone listen to you, you might ask the question, what am I avoiding?

Is it your sense of isolation, your sense of not being approved of or valued? When we talk to people and are addicted to our talking, are we not avoiding these feelings and experiences?

When you are addicted to your cellphone, checking for texts and checking Facebook endlessly, what are you avoiding: your emptiness, pain, isolation, alienation, the pain of boredom? I think that often it's all of the above and yet we don't want to examine or work with or transform these emotions.

And what you avoid disempowers you!

WHAT IS REAL POWER?

We are powerful when we do not constantly respond to the world as though it is an endless threat to us.

I described in the introduction how we go into the Victim position endlessly because the world isn't giving us what we want. As soon as we want something from the world we are at risk of being disempowered, because we cannot tolerate the fact that we are not in control of the world.

Real power is having a solid, strong centre that is balanced and does not require the external world to be a certain way in order to maintain a balance.

It is maintaining one's energy system, whatever the world does or says to us – being able to function at full capacity.

One's internal energy system maintains its integrity and sense of wholeness, *irrespective of what the outside world or reality is doing!*

Stock markets are fascinating. They are highly neurotic and disempowered. They respond to the slightest emotional blip on the economic and political landscape.

Real power – Original Self-Esteem – is not disempowered by the cup that falls and breaks on the floor, by the burnt toast, by Monday mornings, by difficult people and bad service, by incompetence, by illness, by angry people, by traffic jams, by power outages, by cellphones and PCs and tablets that freeze and get viruses and go on the blink and break, by old age, death and loss, by global warming, by corrupt governments.

> *Real power is Mastery, it is not the Victim. It maintains its stature, its internal and external form and shape, its energetic signature, in the face of challenge and threat.*

Most psychological problems are a sign of a loss of power – and love. To my surprise, when I started to do this work I began to realise that even grief can be, to a significant extent – please note, not entirely – a loss of power. Why?

Because grief is saying: "I cannot survive without you. I cannot survive the pain or the loss of not being with you and having you around. I am not a complete person without you and so, because you are gone, I feel incomplete, as though something is missing."

We give away our power to another person so that they can make us happy and so unhappy.

But happiness is not ours to give away.

True happiness is generated internally.

And yes, in terms of this definition, very few people live in a state of true happiness.

I certainly don't, not completely, not yet!

Power does not need anyone else or anything outside of it to enable one to feel complete. Power is independent. Now I know that this might sound like it is disconnected or alienated, but it's not.

Real power is deeply connected to everything and to everyone,

but not from a place of incompleteness.

We don't really have good models for this in our culture, the sense that we can connect with something from a place of completeness and power. But it is possible, and most people have experienced this at least for certain periods of time or in certain moments.

When we are generating our own energy, our own life force, and we are not dependent on someone else's approval or external success or having things our own way in order to generate a sense of goodness, or peace or happiness, then we are truly in a place of Power and it is only really from this place that we can truly interact from a place of love.

What our society most of the time calls love is really not love at all. It is need and want. Byron Katie has the most beautiful phrase:

"The personality doesn't love, it wants."

And she's right.

When we say we love something or someone, we usually mean that they, or it, gratifies us, makes us feel good, and this good feeling is then called love.

So what is my definition of power?

Power is strength and vitality determined internally.

It is maintained, irrespective of external events and physical experiences.

Power knows what it wants and acts spontaneously to get it in a wise and skilful way, but doesn't *have to* get what it wants. Which means that every time we judge ourselves, we lose our vitality and our power, and as soon as we judge other people, we lose our vitality and power, because the judgment is saying we cannot tolerate that which is happening outside of us. So power both loves and accepts what is and yet can transform and influence what is.

When we are powerless, we are at the mercy of our thoughts, feelings and sensations and the world.

There is another really extraordinary experience I had that I want to share with you.

I had just moved into a new housing estate with my partner, Sue, after discovering this work. There was a lot of building happening all around us, as new landowners were constructing their homes. One of our neighbours had a builder who was not particularly liked by anybody. In fact, I had to negotiate an issue around water drainage from their property and spoke to one of the other builders about collaborating with this difficult builder on the issue. His response was an incredibly resistant "No, I don't want to talk to **him** thank you, he's a nutcase!"

His resistance was enormous and he was not the only person who had a problem with this builder – I did too!

I watched myself avoiding having this meeting, making excuses to myself for a number of weeks in order to delay the meeting, and then I realised that I was completely outside of my power in this avoidance.

So I did the work and connected with my power, dissolving all of my resistance and anxiety to meeting with him and walked over to see him.

My experience shocked me.

I found myself **liking** him, and we had the most wonderful and amicable meeting. In fact, I couldn't wait to go back a week or so later to just see him and discuss the progress of his building.

Which raises a really interesting question: how much do we dislike things, situations and people because we are disempowered around them rather than actually having a basic and **real** dislike for them?

In other words, is the dislike actually a rationalised defence against the fact that we don't want to go into a feeling of disempowerment which that person or situation evokes in us?

This is really a fascinating concept and has immense implications. If many of the things we dislike have nothing to do with like or dislike, we are deluding ourselves. Delusion is a prison. To dissolve the delusion is freedom.

I must emphasise that this isn't always the case. Liking and disliking is human. It's real and necessary for survival in many instances. I am simply saying that you can begin to explore whether the dislike is always *primary?*

If you dislike something, or some situation or person, check if you are in your power. If not, then get into your power – which I describe how to do in Part 2 of this book – *and notice if the disliking diminishes.*

If it does, then the issue may have nothing to do with like or dislike; it's about power!

Your teenage son might be playing grunge music. Smiling, you might say: "I don't like it because it disempowers me, him listening to something I think is bad for him."

If you get into your power, perhaps it won't matter what he listens to.

In this instance there may be a real dislike of grunge *and* a disempowerment about the music and your son's love of it, simultaneously!

Any form of stress or pressure that disables our strength, vitality or energy is expressed as powerlessness, whether we go into being underpowered or overpowering.

TRAUMA

I've spent many years as a trauma specialist. I will share with you the two best definitions I know of trauma.

> *"Helplessness in the face of physical threat or injury or death."*
>
> *"An anxious and incomplete response to physical or emotional threat."*
>
> *Adapted from Peter Levine.*

The first definition is fairly straightforward. We hate feeling help-less. Helplessness regresses us emotionally. We feel infantile or childlike *and* we think we might die! This is traumatic stress.

The second definition is slightly different. It is saying that the helplessness is because we cannot respond to the threat. That action or activity is blocked. The problem is that there are so many situations in our lives over which we have no control and where we do not have the ability to *respond!*

We spend hours in meetings and dealing with other people and situations which are completely beyond our control *and which are threatening* and which we have very little or no influence over, and so we become immensely stressed.

In summary, being unable to respond to things over which we don't have control can *disempower* us, leading to a collapse in our Self-Esteem.

The problem is that we spend much of our lives telling stories about how awful the world is and how awful other people are and how problematic they are, because we are trying to control something that is beyond our control *with the mind.*

Indulging in our stories can be immensely disempowering.

CHAPTER 2

The Mind and its Insanity

Where did this mind come from?
This 24/7, unstoppable, thought sprouting factory.
It's unending and unceasing in its self-driven mania.
It is our great tormentor.
It drives us to insanity and back again.
It is contradictory, infantile, paranoid, neurotic and incessant.
At times it is beautiful and creative and inspired and delightful.
Oh this double sided, desperate thing
So indefinable, so irascible, so incomprehensible.
Will I ever tame it and bring it to heal?
This I know not and for now I do not need to know
For it is the mind itself, so ironic, that wants to know!

Mark Peter Kahn.

Obviously, the mind has a multitude of very positive and magnificent qualities.

It has created the most incredible world of technology that surrounds us in all of its forms. It is able to solve problems in the most magnificent of ways, yet the downsides of the mind are immense. It is always creating stories to explain and gain control intellectually of a world over which we have very little control.

In the last couple of years there have been a lot of airline accidents in the news, filled with family members desperately wanting, no demanding, that the airline give them more information, telling them why the plane crashed and what went wrong.

The agony on the faces of these people is overwhelming and this agony is a loss of power.

The pain of the loss of a family member is so great that the mind becomes the tool that is used in an attempt to heal the pain, by finding out why the plane crashed. This search for intellectual understanding is fruitless and pointless and agonising.

It is just an attempt to gain intellectual control over the emotions.

And most importantly *it reflects a loss of power.*

I see people do this in precisely the same way when their intimate partner walks out of the door.

The Self-Esteem that cannot tolerate the pain of the loss looks for another route that is essentially disempowering.

If you make the statement that you cannot live without another person, then you are in Acquired Self-Esteem, because your wholeness and power does not exist without the presence of that person. I hope you can see that, despite the fact that it might seem really strange, grief can, in fact, be healed through regaining Original Self-Esteem. If you begin to find the power and love inside of you without that person, then you have transformed your experience of that loss.

In essence, the mind is used in an attempt to gain control of the pain and disempowerment, but, largely speaking, it fails. The mind is just not very well-suited to this kind of job.

I watch people do this work. I watch them attempt to go back to using the mind to create rationalising stories that they've been using their whole lives, in order to avoid pain. In my opinion, this is the most common mistake that people endlessly make.

So I've heard people say: "Don't give this person rental space in your mind."

As though the mind is able to decide to stop using itself to solve the problem *simply by talking to itself!*

This hardly ever works.

I think we keep doing it, first because it does occasionally work, but also because we don't have any other method, and so if you have only one tool with which to bang in a nail, even if it's only a squash ball, then you are going to keep using that tool.

It's not surprising that we overuse the mind in this way, because First World culture really worships the mind. Descartes's statement "I think, therefore I am" has truly become the sine qua non – the essential ingredient – of the survival of our culture.

So we think that the mind is the only way to do it.

A really beautiful piece of work that I will talk about in a later chapter is around the projection of innocence onto animals. I was working with a client recently who said she couldn't feel the innocence in herself and the way she was trying to access innocence was through the mind.

This is like trying to catch a memory and put it in a bottle so that one can look at it every day. Of course, photographs do a vaguely adequate job of this.

Innocence is an experience that is totally outside of the mind.

Just look at the innocence in the eyes of your cat or dog. There's no thinking going on there, right?

Trying to capture the sense of what innocence is by thinking about it is like trying to get a TV picture on a radio. It will never, never, ever happen.

Innocence is discovered in the body through feeling and intuition and sensation. In fact when we truly feel our innocence, the mind stops and the experience of consciousness in the body and sensation and feeling expands into awareness. This is a very beautiful and incredibly *powerful* experience.

And that is the point.

When we are using the mind to understand something that cannot be understood we are immersing ourselves in disempowerment and a loss of Self-Esteem. When we go outside of the mind, as we have to, in order to access innocence, we experience the most extraordinary power.

If we believe that thinking is our identity, then we believe that only "thought" has power.

What we fail to notice is how often we are disempowered because we are thinking.

And, I'm smiling as I write this because of the absurdity, the insanity that is so apparent as I picture us human beings using the mind fruitlessly – as in the case of the airline disaster survivors – and not seeing the disempowerment that it brings.

But it's not only regarding airline disasters that we use the mind inappropriately.

We do this every day of our lives in a multitude of different ways. We try to understand why customer service is so bad or why our partner doesn't *do* something about the job they hate or the headaches the they keep getting, or why corporations don't care about the environment or why politicians behave so badly, or why their kids are so disrespectful and think they know it all, or why life is so difficult … and on and on and on the list goes.

I am endlessly confronted by clients who are constantly trying to use their minds to manage their emotions, and the mind just isn't good at this.

They try to use their minds to manage hurt, and guilt, and sadness, and shame, and aggression, and they fail, endlessly they fail, not 100% of the time, but most of the time. (If we failed 100% of the time, we would probably give it up!)

And so this work is offering you another tool. In addition to using power and love and innocence and trust to dissolve negative emotions.

My experience both personally and professionally is that we settle for so little in our lives. We settle for a powerlessness that we do not even notice because we do not notice all the forms that powerlessness takes. If you begin to see all of the ways in which you disempower yourself on a daily basis, quite apart from all of the major issues in life that we struggle with, then anything is possible.

There is a power residing inside of you that is waiting to be claimed. All you have to do is the work, to see it grow.

SURVIVAL

The mind's primary job is to enable this organism to survive and to do so it must essentially be vigilant, on the lookout for danger.

It does this in order to survive. Animals in the wild do this very well without a very sophisticated mental apparatus and they're not hypervigilant, just simply aware and awake to the potential for danger.

There is that wonderful book by Robert Sapolsky, *Why zebras don't get ulcers.*

And the reason is that zebras do not have a ruminative mind, endlessly worrying about everything.

Zebras don't worry endlessly about when the next lion is going to attack.

We human beings are unfortunately paranoid. We use the mind to endlessly look out for what's missing, what's a problem, what's dangerous and what's safe.

The mind of a human being is not very good at discriminating between what is truly a danger and what is a figment of the imagination or what is just an irritation or a minor hurdle. When it comes to "thinking", everything is food for paranoia, doubt, criticism and the endless need to approve and disapprove of all that it encounters.

Now we get to something really important. There are, broadly speaking, three types of thinking:

- Ruminative thinking.
- Ego-trip thinking.
- Creative, problem-solving and wise thinking.

RUMINATIVE THINKING

Ruminative thinking is almost entirely destructive. By now you are aware of the amount of time we spend in a ruminative state, *chewing our thoughts over and over and over again* in a way that is non-productive, paranoid, anxiety producing and Self-Esteem reducing.

There are, however, occasions when it does seem to lead to creative thought. It's as though the mind exhausts itself and creative thought sometimes seems to simply burst through into awareness.

What is really interesting is that an increase in power and love can reduce the *tendency* to ruminate.

I say "tendency" with particular emphasis, because raised Self-Esteem is probably not going to eliminate ruminative thought entirely. But it will almost certainly reduce it.

The reason is that many, though not all, of our ruminations are based on anxiety and a need to control outcomes of events. Reduce the anxiety and the need to control, and the ruminations are going to reduce as well.

The mind is an absolute genius at judging *everything!*

I'd like to explore this further.

The thought "I'm selfish" is what I call a first-order judgement.

Then comes: "Stop judging yourself, Mark!" A second-order judgement. A judgmental reflection on the fact that I have just judged myself.

And finally the ruminative reflection: "I've been judging myself for years and I can't stop, I'm a failure, I'm not worthy, I'm not good enough!" The third-order judgement.

At the third level, we are making global, overarching judgements that reflect the themes of the calcified suffering that we inflict upon ourselves for decades, until we die. To put it another way, third-order judgements are the Big Picture assessments that we have of ourselves: "I'm a failure, I'm a bad person, I'm ugly, I'm needy, nobody will ever want me, nobody truly loves me, I'm unlovable, I'm only lovable if I have good reasons to be so."

This is the deepest and most destructive level of Self-Esteem, and it is so often the theme of most people's lives.

Just about everybody does first- or second-order judgements. The people we consider to be happiest are probably those who do less of the third-order judging.

All judgements have at their base a need to establish and maintain a sense of identity that is good and laudable. This is what we all are trained to do and it causes us immense pain. The self-conscious and endless reflections on what and who we are, breed suffering.

To discover that you are something beyond this identity that is interminably judged, is an immense blessing.

EGO-TRIP THINKING

Ego-trip thinking creates many nightmares.

It's all about how can I frame this argument to win, to beat you into submission, to conquer, to be the victor, to not let you beat me, to not fail, to not look bad, incompetent...?

How can I get more pleasure and less pain. Do I approve of you or this, or not?

It is divisive; it is about superiority and pleasure and nothing else. If peace and serenity are wholeness, ego-trip thinking splits the whole into parts and it wants to be the part that wins.

Ego-trip thinking is competitive, and we love competition: the Olympics, the world cups, Apple vs Microsoft vs Samsung, Ford vs Chevrolet, which is the most productive country, best economy, best city to live in, most expensive vs the cheapest city, the best singer, the sexiest person, the richest person ... the list is endless. It is the very fabric of our First World culture.

Many years ago there was a really clever BMW advert. It simply said: "I want it because I want it!" That's the ego trip, addicted to what it wants.

What was so clever about the advert was that it was giving legitimacy to the making of an ego-trip purchase, without having to feel guilty!

Ego-trip thinking infiltrates the area where we expect logic and reason to be king: the arena of science. But the ego will hijack anything, and in the realm of scientific research the ego is rampant. Mavericks are not well tolerated.

Ego-trip thinking obviously overlaps significantly with ruminative thinking.

CREATIVE THINKING, PROBLEM SOLVING & WISE THINKING

In the arena of creative problem-solving, the mind is really very useful. Everything that distinguishes us from our days as cavemen and women has been created by or at least through the mind.

The invention of the wheel, the use of fire, the creation of electricity and the ability to store and deliver water to homes and offices and factories, the ability to manufacture boats and planes and motorcars and PCs and the internet and to write books and to test and make use of scientific theories, to create music and art and the endless multitude of necessities and luxuries that are so much a part of our lives, and, not least of all, the advances in medicine.

All of this is part of the magic and magnificence of the mind. But, as I have mentioned, double-sidedness emerges.

And so the mind has all these upsides, but the downsides are its ruminative and ego-trip nature. Most of our neurosis is a result of these two negative qualities, and they can be very destructive indeed.

What I have observed so frequently in people and my clients is that they are brilliant at using the mind for problem solving, in their work, in their careers, but when they try to use the mind to understand why, for example, their partner is ignoring them, or they try to rationalise away their fear of public speaking, this simply results in ruminative paranoia and increased levels of anxiety, disconnection and inappropriate expression of anger.

To put it another way, the mind is very powerful when used in the right place at the right time. It is *disempowering* when used in the wrong place at the wrong time.

Can you begin to notice where you are using your mind and it is functional and productive and where you are using it and it is destructive?

Your ability to dissolve the need to use it when it is not helpful is immensely empowering. *Cultivating Wisdom*, which I will be talking about shortly, enables this capacity.

In addition to all of the above, what the mind cannot do is connect with pure consciousness or spirit or soul. The mind can only divide, distinguish, pick apart, analyse and dissect. And when it is doing this, it cannot find consciousness, because the latter *includes* everything. Consciousness is an experience. Thought is outside of an experience, analysing it.

In the meditative aspects of this work, you will connect with consciousness that is already here. In doing so, you will connect with Original Self-Esteem, which is outside of thought, outside of self-consciousness.

There is a vast difference between Consciousness and Self-Consciousness. Escaping the grasp of the latter is liberation. It is love. The mind cannot love. It might have loving thoughts, but love is experienced in the heart, in the body ... a long way from the mind.

CHAPTER 3

A Love Poem

AUDIO RECORDING

You can access an audio recording of this poem. If you're reading this as an eBook, you can click on the link below to access the recording. If you are reading this on a hardcopy, type the link into your web browser to access the audio.

http://bit.ly/poemsmeditations

How can I possibly live a life like this?
Where my mind is the King, the Supreme Boss, God of all things,
Where no error, no mistake, no mis-step,
no imperfection will be tolerated,
Where this ever paranoid eye of mine
Will seek out and blame and eviscerate the lifeblood from me,
In a logical rage of vicious condemnation.

How can I possibly live a life like this?
How can I possibly survive in a world like this?
In which a reason is demanded for everything,
Where I have to defend my-self, my being-
ness, my true and unique nature
From attack and judgement,
As though the attackers knew the truth,
As though I am not perfect as I am,
Not lovable as I am.

How can I possibly survive in a world like this?

How can I possibly go on living in a world like this?
Both outside and inside of my mind,
They are mirror images, meeting in ravaged pain.
Through the conditioning, the training, the manipulation,
The bullying, the control, the authoritarian
judgments and edicts,
Visited with subterranean guile and overt barbarity,
Upon my Spirit, upon my sensitive and gentle being.
How can I possibly go on living in a world like this?

Do I have to go on living like this?
Under the shadow of this tyranny, this scourge
This King of barbarous subterfuge and logic,
Scoring me, rating me, measuring me, adjudicating me,
Ego tripping me up – side down, head over heels,
Tumbled, snowballed down the mountain,
Ragged edged, bleeding, crying,
moaning, suffering and longing,
Just to be loved.
But it will never come through eyes looking outwards.
As long as I seek and long and look and
pine and drive myself into
Pitted hell, dreaming, screaming for everlasting love…
Do I have to go on living like this?

Can I conceivably go on like this?
Stacking up reasons that make me sublime
And then this mind begins to list,
Each and every slip and sway away from perfection.
Undaunted and daunted I continue to chase
That which is outside always, of reach.
"Reason is God," said René Descartes, my mind wants to argue
But it fights with itself, this civil-mind-war
is endless so sad, exhausting,
Reason is everything, it's how the rules are writ, the race is run,

But down so ever deep in our hearts, we know what's true,
How can we listen, so acutely, to this
beautiful yet so refined voice,
To just relax, let go, to know that we are love,
Before and during and after all things
Have come to pass and have passed away.
Can I conceivably go on like this?

Do I want to go on like this?
I'm oh so clever and oh so stupid
Oh so giving and oh so selfish,
Oh so beautiful and oh so ugly,
Oh so kind and oh so cruel,
Oh so honest and such a liar,
A merry-go-round of loved and abused
And as 'being loved' dissolves so fast,
The grip of fear in my gut expands
A Gordian knot of hell,
That aches and tears my being apart
"Who will love this pain away?" again I ask.
"What good fortune will dissolve this dread?"
I do this to myself, for I've learned the script so well,
Freedom awaits but I live enchained by
these conditioned rules of self-rape!
That convince me to believe my draconian
judgements of self and other.
Do I want to go on like this?

What would it feel like to no longer go on like this?
To believe the inane and insane thoughts of my mind,
That nuke my Esteem, in this internal holocaust,
Of hatred and destruction.
I give away my power
To those who commit the same crime within and without.
What would it feel like to no longer go on like this?

What has become of this love I once was?

Lost in the grasping, gasping, clawing for pleasure,
Running, hiding, resisting all hurts...
To stop for a moment, to see that love is here
Amidst the pleasure and the pain,
Beyond and within the pleasure and the pain,
This ephemeral love.
What has become of this love I once was?

In the endless 'doings' of my life.
As I walk down the street, I drive my car, I eat, make love,
Sleep, stand in queues, clear my inbox, create, negate,
Strive and drive to control all things,
Waiting for love to happen.
Can I see in the midst of it all,
Silently in the centre, waiting, a pin point of light
That is as great as the power of a thousand suns,
Enshrouded in clasping, agonised longing,
Waiting with infinite and endless patience to emerge.
In the endless 'doings' of my life.

Could I possibly stop doing this?
You look at me with disapproval,
I hurt you, reject you, criticise you.
Guilt is the harbour in which I anchor my boat
I was late, I was frustrated, I was selfish.
Self-flagellation is what you want of me
Anxiety attacks me because I believe your rules.
I create my own rules that bleed me.
How good I must be?
Is this a lie I've been seduced by?
How to escape...into love...
But how-to-love-myself.
Could I possibly do this?

Could I conceivably dissolve the doing of this?
And simply love myself for no reason?
Is this too foreign a language?

Too far from the shores of conditioning
you force fed me, slaved me in,
This fragile, wide eyed, so pristine pure,
So beautiful cherubed child that I was,
So helpless, so innocent, so gullible, so trusting in you
That I gave you my power, leaked myself dry and empty
Of love and courage,
Could I conceivably dissolve the doing of this?

What would it feel like to know that I was love, for no reason?
To soften and open like a petalled flower in the springtime sun,
Unleashing the fire of love in infinite
and abundant beauty and joy,
Oh what would it feel like,
To know that all of the lies that judged me
Were as insubstantial
As the mist in morning valleys,
As the dew dried up by the day's heat,
As the puffed white clouds disappearing into the blue,
As a momentary thought, floating across
the confines of my mind?
Can I burn these lies in the fire of my heart,
Crucibled heat expanding into Phoenix rising,
Dancing into wordless space, unspoken delight?
Oh what would it feel like to love myself for no reason?

I enter the Gateway,
Liberty, freedom, un-chained and joyous
I rest outside of thought, concept, cognition, logic,
A realm of light so bright,
I'm speechless, transcendent and oh so Still.
I enter the Gateway.

Can I love myself in the face of your reasons why not to?
The greatest test is this.
The compulsion to agree with external judgements
Is like the power of the word of truth, of God,

Spoken from the sacred mountain.
And we have believed and gone on believing,
Because we need to be loved so badly…it crucifies us.
The mountain is made of nothing, a monolithic mirage,
Thoughts, beliefs, words, diaphanous,
Riding on the back of a cold, false wind.
Can I love myself in the face of your reasons why not to?

Can I love and let be, everything that is?
I'm hurt, affronted, offended, inadequate, lonely, doubtful,
Anxious – ever so anxious…endlessly anxious,
Frustrated, opinionated, deflated and depressed, negative
And lost, filled with longing and doubt, certainty and prejudice,
Can I love all of this that I am and let it all be?

To fall, trusting, backwards into the well of love within
Is the antidote.
This is salvation, resurrection
Reborn in the love from which we once died,
Into Pure Consciousness.

Can I stop for a moment, sensing that there is a Universe,
Beyond the mindless mind, turmoiled incessant,
Just sitting, doing nothing,
No doer, just exquisite doing, not needing
a 'me' to make it happen,
To drive and motivate and push and strive,
To manufacture a being-ness that is already here.
The Prodigal, returning home,
In tears of joy and peace.

Mark Peter Kahn.

CHAPTER 4

Activating Love & Power

You have been trained to give love to others, but not to give it to yourself.

This is a tragedy of immense proportions.

It means you are doomed to search for love on the outside and you will only have moments of finding it. You will be endlessly searching and blaming and judging life and the world for not giving you enough of it.

You will continue to chase after more loving relationships *and people will endlessly let you down.*

And you will be endlessly fantasising about how you will get it from experiences or from your career.

And all fantasies are lies. We are lying to ourselves.

As regards power, we give it away and we forget that we ever had it.

FORGOTTEN RESILIENCE

Some years ago I created a series of workshops in a company, with some colleagues, around building resilience. One of the most significant things I learned in doing this work was that most people forget their resilience and their powerful experiences of the past.

We are confronted by a difficulty, a challenge, a trauma and we somehow do not recall the power and strength that we experienced previously when confronted by something similar.

Sometimes we experience power ... and then we dump it. We go into shock, resentment, vulnerability and helplessness again and again when confronted by situations that we previously coped with really well.

It is as though this reservoir of strength and capacity becomes removed or very distant from our consciousness.

This is really unfortunate, because when we coped well and managed a crisis skilfully, we built our Self-Esteem. So, if what we have built disappears from view or is simply not available for us to access, we lose the value of that experience.

And, of course, if it disappears from view, we think that it is outside of us and so we look to other people and fantasise about things that need to happen in order to make us feel good. And remember: "It isn't money that makes the world go around; it's your fantasies."

And so I have the expression:

"If you could connect with and stay with all of the love and power in yourself that you have ever known and that you truly are, you would never need it from anyone else."

THE INTERCONNECTEDNESS OF POWER & LOVE

Power is about accomplishment, pride, strength, a sense of worth, feeling validated and competent, strong and *energised*. The word "energised" is italicised because it is about experiencing energy in the body that is so important.

The receiving of love is where you felt special, validated, appreciated, empathised with, and where you received compassion, warmth and kindness. All of these qualities are interrelated. Feeling loved can lead to feeling powerful, although not usually vice versa.

What is most important is that when you love yourself and know that you are love, this specialness, this vast well of warmth inside you, is just there spontaneously, before thought.

LOVE AS INSPIRATION

Some years ago I listened to an Olympic athlete being interviewed after the Games. He had just missed the bronze medal and was disappointed, but described his experience of being at the Olympics in more or less the following way:

"It was truly a wonderful experience. It was such a privilege to be in the company of truly great athletes and I learned so much from them. I really know now what I need to do to get to the next level, to take my capacity to the level to really be great. It was a really a transformative experience."

You can hear the depth of joy and inspiration in this quote. When our Original Nature, our love shines forth, it is inspiration and joy.

If he was just happy and excited, he would've said something like:

"It was just amazing, it was so wonderful. I had a fantastic time. Just the atmosphere and the energy of the place. I was really on a high most of the time. I can't wait to get back to try and do better."

Can you hear in this second instance how the feelings lacks substance, breadth and depth and they have a sense of impatience about them? "I can't wait to get back..."?

They are coming from a short-lived, narrow place that does not have a real power.

It is really interesting to note how much of the time in our society we talk from this 'second position' example. And when we do this, we limit ourselves, and our lives are experienced with less depth and resonance because of it.

Power and love are different words, but there is a lot of overlap between them. It is possible to be very, very powerful without being loving or joyful. Hitler, Stalin, Idi Amin were leaders with a great deal of power, but I think we'd all agree that there was little love or joy in them. So power can tend to be a discreet entity, standing alone.

Indeed, one of the things that accessing your power can do is push you into self-righteousness and arrogance and, in fact, into becoming overpowering. It is not uncommon for people who spend a lot of time in their lives in the disempowered position to move to the opposite extreme, which is overpowering.

If this happens to you, accept that this is a natural overcompensation and work to bring yourself into the centre.

Always remember that power sits in the balanced position in the middle between disempowered and overpowering.

Most people commit what I call a *binary error*. It's an "all-or-nothing" way of perceiving the world. They see only the two ends of a continuum. I'm overpowering or disempowered. I'm superior or inferior. I'm aggressive or passive.

They miss power, self-love, assertiveness as the middle points in the continuum.

Love is extremely powerful, and so there's an overlapping here between love and power. The power of love is experienced in its ability to transmit an energy that is uplifting and transforming and healing, both within and from other people. Love is infectious and so too can power be positively infectious.

In the resilience company that I talked about earlier, I'll never forget an experience I had one day when we were about to have a partners' meeting. Three of us were sitting waiting for the fourth to arrive and there was an energy in the room of anxiety and deflation. The company was in its start-up phase and there were many challenges and difficulties, and on that particular afternoon the three of us were not feeling particularly good.

And then our fourth partner walked into the room with the most tremendous energy and excitement about a meeting she had just had around this work and completely transformed the energy in the room. Her power lifted us and energised us all. It truly was an inspired and inspiring energy.

And of course it's almost superfluous to say that love and power are infectious. And certainly we can be loving and joyful at the same time, and this can be very powerful too.

What all this means is that these three qualities interlink and interweave in a beautiful way. Work on all three of them and notice how they impact your life. In general, Original Self-Esteem, if cultivated and developed everywhere, has the capacity to transform the world.

POWER AS A NOUN

When I talk about Power and Love it's important to notice that I am talking about them as nouns and verbs.

In this book, I'm describing the feeling that one *is* love, as a noun – a thing – which simply radiates, as its natural being, an energy of love. When we discover the love that we are, we are like the sun, just shining with love, a noun – a thing – and a verb – that does something. And again, this is often expressed as inspiration.

It might be tricky at first for you to feel that you *are* love and so you might need to have the sense that you are being loved and then generating love and finally that you *are* love. The meditative process I will be working with enables the discovery that we are love, while the psychological processes enable one to *do* the loving of oneself.

It is the same with power. We are power, the noun, and we act powerfully, the verb.

What is also very interesting is that I've worked with many people who have focused on developing their spiritual capacity, deepening their experience of what it means to transform spiritually, and many of them have attained a greater sense of Stillness or Peace or Tranquility, but have still been disempowered in many ways. As one of my clients said to me in doing this work, "I'm experiencing the Stillness, but now it's infused with power."

This is really important and very beautiful, because it is possible to experience Stillness at the level of mind but nevertheless to be disempowered, at the level of the gut, in relation to the rest of the world.

WHAT DOES LOVING YOURSELF MEAN IN PRACTICE?

"Most people are empty of love on the inside. That is why they are victims of events on the outside."

To love yourself for no reason looks like this:

- It means that when you have a conflict at work, you are not driving home, telling the story about it in your head to your partner, so that they can fill up the deficit of love inside of you.

- It means that when you are sitting around doing nothing in particular you are filled with love.

- It means that when you are watching a movie on TV you are so filled with love that if the movie isn't good enough, you don't get distressed. If you get distressed because the movie is disappointing, you are wanting the movie to fill you with love because there isn't enough of that on the inside.

- You've had a great day and you are looking forward to seeing your partner when they get home and they are in a bad mood and it freaks you out. It's because there is not enough love on the inside to enable you to love them in their bad mood.

- Your partner or friend or business associate does something irritating or they are difficult or boring or repetitive or simply push your buttons. If you are filled with love, it's not a problem.

- You or someone else gets ill or has an accident or someone close to you dies. If you freak out, then there's not enough love inside of you to contain this issue.

- If you have money issues and career issues and problems with people and that upset you, it's okay.

- If somebody tries to overpower you or bully you, you don't let them.

- You can say no without any excuse or defence.

- You don't have to justify your likes, dislikes, your personality.

I recently broke a contract because I felt that I was not being valued in a relationship. A friend of mine felt that I was being brutal and not giving the person involved time to dialogue the issue with me. I didn't have time. I needed to be brutal.

I honoured the trait of brutality inside of me and I want to thank Dr Demartini for bringing this concept to my awareness.

This was loving myself. I use this example because most of us perceive brutality as really bad.

It's not. It's useful. That's why we have it. To act really fast and brutally got me what I needed for my work, my business and supported my values.

I chose to be brutal. It was, in my perception, wise action. The problem occurs when the trait is controlling you. I was in control of the trait. I love my capacity to act out this trait when needed.

I love this trait in me!

To love yourself is to love your brutality, your selfishness, your manipulativeness, your laziness, your callousness ... all of it!

• You still love yourself when you are selfish, manipulative, tell lies, are unkind, distant, a bad father, mother, partner, employee, lazy ... whatever! This is so important. We have expectations on ourselves that require us to be outside of the definition of human. To love yourself, is to love your human imperfections, full stop.

Indeed, perhaps they are not imperfections.

The biggest driving force on the planet is human beings wanting things to happen and thinking that they should happen.

What this means is that we think that wanting things and getting them will make us happy.

It doesn't, except temporarily.

We also think that we *should* get what we want. This is an inordinately powerful belief.

The belief drives us crazy. If we believe that we should be able to make an intimate relationship work, or be rich, or be more physically attractive, whatever it is, we either consider ourselves a failure or get frustrated and depressed because this "should" doesn't come true.

We want to be masters of the universe and it impossible.

For most people, failure is a major problem. But failure is a concept.

When one-year-olds learn to walk, they walk, fall down, walk, fall down ... endlessly.

They don't have the concept of failure. They don't say: "I'll never be able to walk so well like you grown-ups. You can even run! Oh dear, I'm such a failure at this!" So they don't give up and they don't get depressed about it.

Failure doesn't exist, except as a concept, and a concept is just a thought; it's not the truth.

If you can get into the consciousness of the child that doesn't yet have the concept of failure, you're free. Then life is just living itself without this driving *wanting* and "shoulding".

Fill yourself with love and power, and life's difficulties – which are endless – are no longer so threatening or overwhelming. Love is there, not matter what happens.

"The reason we struggle to have loving relationships is that for much of the time ... we just aren't loving!"

Byron Katie has *the* most beautiful phrase. She says:

> *"In my world, 'Do I love you?' is the only important question.*
> *'Do you love me?' is a prison. It's a torture chamber."*

When our relationships are threatened, what do we do? We look at our partner and we make a list of things that are wrong with them. Essentially we are listing the ways in which they aren't loving us and that's the prison, the torture chamber.

When you love yourself enough, you are not interested in whether the person is loving you but you are looking at what is in the way of you loving them. This is freedom from the prison that is always looking to get more love on the outside and endlessly failing.

Our neurotic needs are so painful and so overpowering that mostly we can't look within and love ourselves, so our next best option is to look externally ... and blame.

> *The reason we struggle to have loving relationships is*
> *that much of the time, we are just ... not loving.*

This might sound simplistic, but it's not. Most people get into intimate relationships to feel gratified by them. Forget it. Your partner is going to push every button inside of you. When they do, you're probably not going to behave in a loving way, and so conflict and alienation ensue.

In addition, as "wanting machines" we are looking to have our partner gratify our wants, as opposed to us *loving* them. The only way I know around this is to heal your pain and learn to activate love and power internally, and that transforms everything.

Go to Chapter 16 for the strategy.

CHAPTER 5

FROM PAIN TO LOVE & POWER - 1.0

I am an adult.
I walk into a room of strangers
It is as though I have walked onto a battlefield.
My eyes dart back and forth,
My heart pounds,
My gut contracts
I search for safety and strain against
My brutal anxiety.
It is as though I am about to be stabbed.
No - my paranoia stabs me before anyone stabs me..

I see the world through the pain of my past
It is as alive in me today as it was those
decades ago when I was a child.
Tiny, smaller than a grain of sand lost
in a desert of excruciating size
The wicked lashes of words stinging my heart
Staining my mind.
Time contracts
It's all here right now
This agony.

There is no now,
I am past, present and future
Aflame with poisoned darts of wounded, bleeding fear.

Mark Peter Kahn.

Pain to Power 1.0 is dealing with our past. 2.0 is dealing with the pain in the present.

There is no question that the pain we have experienced in the past controls our lives in the present. This can become so much a part of our existence that we hardly notice it. It is, in a sense, unconscious and "un-see-able".

Everybody has pain, and past pain creates disempowerment in the present. Let me explain.

Let us say for example that you didn't do particularly well at school. It embarrassed you. You didn't feel clever enough. Your parents pressured you and threatened you and challenged you to do better.

You wanted to do better, but you were depressed and deflated and so you didn't really work hard enough. Your sense of inadequacy floated through your psyche and through your body endlessly and constantly. It became the background to your existence. It made you doubt yourself and believe that you were not okay. It made you hesitant in relationships and you would often flee into what I call retreat in order to escape criticism and rejection from others.

The sensitivity to rejection was really based on the fact that you were rejecting yourself because of your failures and giving away your self-worth to your parents who judged you and because you were *believing* what your parents said about you. The sense that they gave you, that you were not okay because you didn't do well at school, was true, for you.

> *To go on believing for a lifetime everything our parents told us as children is devastating to us.*

When you left school, it still left you feeling doubtful. Although you might have done reasonably well in your career, every time you sat down in the boardroom to discuss some project, some difficulty in the business, your sense that you would be easily rejected was floating in your consciousness – a sensitivity, a vulnerability, a mild paranoia that always left you feeling slightly tense, a little hypervigilant and, here's what's so important, *not fully* in your power and creativity, not fully energised and awake.

Essentially your Self-Esteem was acquired. You only really felt good when you were doing well. The Original Self-Esteem that you were born with occasionally showed itself in moments of freedom and spontaneity, but essentially you were guarded and not *fully yourself.*

What is so interesting about this scenario is that many things could have caused it, not just the fact that you didn't do well enough at school or you didn't feel clever enough generally.

When I behaved "badly" as a kid – at least in my father's perception – he would threaten to call the police. This threat created the most incredible paranoia in me, in really deep and subtle ways, but absolutely pervasively. I spent most of my life going into a deep anxiety around getting into trouble. Being hypervigilant around other people's anger or resentment at me.

Any form of aggression can cause this kind of problem. It pervades the entire personality and, most importantly, much of our behaviour, *particularly when we're under threat of rejection, criticism or fear of abandonment.*

I have met many, many people who claim that the issues of the past are not an issue at all. What they are doing is simply repressing into their unconscious the impact that painful early experiences had on them.

Carolyn Myss a medical intuitive in the United States says most acutely: "We have all had our Self-Esteem raped."

What she might have added is that many, many people have either forgotten the "raping" or they don't see the impact it is having on their lives in the present moment.

Many people develop an emotional and physical armour to protect themselves from the pain of the past. They develop a tough and aggressive exterior to mask this inner pain.

Their tendency is to blame the rest of the world for all of the problems that they have. They don't take responsibility. They don't know that the problem is inside of them. But the deep level of pain and disempowerment within them creates a sense of a bully boy, overpowering attitude on the exterior designed to keep everyone at a distance and to protect the self.

I have shared only one scenario with you above, but it doesn't matter what the scenario of pain from the past is; it is very likely that it haunts you in the present. The more you dissolve this pain, the more the present, that which we are now, transforms into power.

Go to chapter 17 for the strategy.

CHAPTER 6

CULTIVATING WISDOM

The mind has inserted into it
With wicked guile and subterfuge
With threat of love to be withdrawn,
A thousand rules and laws…based on fear.

And never did they disclose,
How wobbly, was this foundation.

Abandoned and marooned
On an island of shame
Your fragile self no longer held
In the arms of your people.

They betrayed you with promises
Of this love.
For to comply with their rules, these straitjackets or conformity,
Left you abandoning the essence, the vitality,
The power and courage and love,
Of your true self.

Mark Peter Kahn.

> *Most of the work is embodied in the theoretical*
> *description as opposed to the 'technique section.'*

There is the most beautiful scene in a movie called *The East*. The heroine has infiltrated a terrorist group that is targeting corporations for their injustices against society.

It is the night of her first dinner with the group. They tell her that she has to wear a straitjacket if she wants to eat dinner with them. She is obviously shocked at this comment and very anxious about doing this, but agrees.

She walks into the dining room in the straitjacket and the rest of the group, about 12 of them, are all sitting round the table of food, with their straitjackets on.

The room is all sombre colours, browns and tans and they all look like young revolutionaries with lots of hair, earnest and filled with missionary zeal.

They instruct the heroine to eat first. She doesn't know what to do. She looks bewildered and confused. The leader of the group says to her in an extraordinarily gentle and calm way: "There's no wrong way to do it."

When I heard these words I was overwhelmed with the mental and emotional realisation of the thousands of times in my life when I had wondered,

"Am I doing this the right way?"

I was incredibly moved, and a spontaneous transformation slowly expanded inside of me. A discovery that there isn't a "right way" to do anything – despite what we've been taught.

I was so deeply aware of the immense pain that I carried inside of me from being controlled and manipulated into doing things the "right way".

This is the conditioning that we all receive from our parents, our teachers, our media and our culture.

So can you ask yourself to what extent this conditioning is running a story inside of you?

I'm not an expert in social anthropology, but I would think that most cultures do this. We train people to do things in a particular way and we call it right, correct and good.

This conditioning is insanity – though it does have its own perverse kind of logic.

There is no right and correct way to do anything! There is the way we *want* people to do things and, yes, we do want people to conform. But is there a "right" way, and why do we want to control each other like this?

In a nutshell, we are addicted to control. And this need for control inhibits our authenticity and spontaneity and it shuts down our Original Self-Esteem and our sense of worth and value. And then we feel bad when we want to do it in a way that is different from somebody else's way.

All of this is the agony, the destruction, the prison of conditioning.

To have some degree of order in society, some conditioning is necessary, but the problem is the violence and lack of skill with which it is inflicted on us.

Is that necessary?

As a child you might be sitting in a chair in your bedroom staring at the wall and your parents walk into the room and they say, angrily, in an accusatory manner: "What are you doing?"

Of course, you are doing nothing, and doing nothing is bad, it's a wrong.

We have the insane expression, "Idle hands are the devil's work!" And so we always have to be *doing* something, we become human *doings* as opposed to human *beings*.

It is part of the insanity of our First World culture.

We don't accuse animals of being bad when they just sit and do nothing, do we?

Which is not to say there are not many magnificent things that come out of this driving, pushing attitude. But what we could learn to do is take the good parts of this First World driving, doing, pushing culture and use it when appropriate and then *let go of it* when it's not appropriate.

But we don't know how to do that ... much.

And so we live in a culture of immense stress.

Irrespective of how good or bad this conditioning is for us, the point is, if you see the pain that the conditioning has created in you and how it has wreaked havoc on your Self-Esteem, you are on the way to transformation.

Returning to the story from the movie.

Eventually the heroine takes the handle of her spoon in her mouth and begins to ladle food into her bowl, very carefully and very slowly. Everyone looks on silently.

She then draws the bowl closer to her, with her teeth and begins to lap up the food like a dog.

Everyone else around the table then places the handle of the spoon in front of them, in their mouths and begins to feed the person next to them!

It is the most exquisite adaptation of a story which I read over 30 years ago in Irvin Yalom's book *Existential Psychotherapy.*

We don't know how to give to each other. Under pressure, our first thought is usually to take care of ourselves rather than to take care of each other, and this is, to some extent, the reason for much of the violence and the destructiveness of our culture.

What is symbolically very significant in the story is the strait-jackets that everyone is wearing.

Conditioning is a straitjacket that we've all been caged in, yet our awareness of it is limited at best.

To cultivate wisdom is to take off the straitjacket of conditioning. It is to dissolve these prison bars that keep us trapped in our pain.

Continuing with the story.

The heroine storms out of the room when she sees everybody feeding their neighbour.

The leader of the group follows her, stops her and says he wants her to stay for the dinner. She very angrily replies: "You made me look like a fool." To which he replies: "Maybe the judgement was yours."

Which again beautifully reflects how we project our own judgments onto others.

I would have taken this dialogue further and I have, in fact, shared this extended dialogue with clients who have found it immensely helpful.

Here is my extended dialogue.

Leader: "You don't think we all made the same mistake you made when we joined this group? And we all thought we were being made a fool of, yes? We all engage in behaviours which we are at times ashamed of and which we judge. Isn't that human nature?"

Heroine: "I never thought about it that way."

Leader: "I know, we never do. When we're threatened and pressured and anxious, we think others are against us and sometimes they are, but firstly and *mostly* we are against ourselves, so that is the teaching. Can you allow yourself to be a human being, fallible, flawed, imperfect and can you not see how your selfishness, under pressure, is what most of us do, most of the time?

"And this is what our group is trying to illustrate about our society. We want to soften the selfishness, the greed. As Mahatma Gandhi said: 'The world has enough for everyone's need, but not for everyone's greed.'"

A CULTURE OF LIES

All of us, to varying degrees, are living in a prison and the bars are, for most of us, invisible. For some, the prison is Super-Max – maximum security. For others, they are lightweight and the prison warders are few and far between. But nevertheless, we are all trained to live in this prison.

And what is this prison comprised of?

Lies.

Lies masquerading as truth, fed into our body-mind by parents, caregivers, teachers, politicians, corporations, the media ... the culture we live in, as well as those created by ourselves.

There is nothing more insidious than a lie that masquerades as the truth.

If the truth shall set you free, then the lie will imprison you.

But what can you do about the lie which you cannot see? We cannot see the flu virus that infects us. We cannot see our high blood pressure or our kidney stones forming. We cannot see our arteries clogged with cholesterol.

And most of the lies living within our belief systems are similarly invisible to us.

What follows in this chapter is my attempt to make the invisible visible, so that you can set yourself free.

DON'T LET THE GUEST SMELL THE MILK!

I had a really fascinating experience recently.

One of my neighbours came around on a Sunday morning to get me to sign a petition to object to a new cellphone tower that was going to be put up in our estate. Making her a cup of coffee, I noticed that the milk smelled sour. I wasn't going to be having any milk myself.

As I smelled the milk I found myself saying: "This smells sour, what do you think?" and handed her the bottle.

As I did this, I realised that somehow or other I was breaking a rule which said:

Don't let the guest smell the milk!

Isn't that strange and fascinating that nobody ever told me directly that I shouldn't let the guest smell the milk yet somehow I had created this belief!

How insane.

It was a piece of conditioning that I had inferred from the way my parents brought me up, but had never been directly said. What is really interesting is that many of the rules that reside in our minds are not given to us explicitly, and *the less explicit they are, the more powerful their impact* because we don't have some specific idiotic injunction to fight directly.

So a parent says to a child with a raised eyebrow, a hand on the hip and a deeply aggressive tone, after the child has bumped his sister: "So you're not going to apologise?"

What the child learns is that inconveniencing or upsetting others is a crime and that to not apologise is to be a criminal. And then they go around the rest of their lives endlessly and constantly apologising, even when there is no need to do so, in order to avoid the guilt that sits inside of their body-mind as a result of this once-off admonition.

I want to share some other "insanity producing" rules that restrict and constrain us, but before I do I want to make a really important point. The way to find what kind of conditioning is running you is to:

> *Notice the rule behind your guilt or anxiety!*

A client said to me one day: "I'm an overachiever, it drives me nuts. I've done very little work today (it was a Wednesday) and I feel really guilty."

So I asked her who told her that it was bad to do nothing on a workday? And she said: "My father, David." So I said to her: "I want you to be David and I'm going to talk to him okay?" She agreed.

Mark: "So David, you believe that people shouldn't sit around all day doing nothing unless perhaps on a Sunday afternoon?"

David: "Yes!"

Mark: "And this has made you a happy person?"

David: "Well, maybe not so happy, but I'm productive."

Mark: "So productivity at the expense of happiness…? This is a very good thing and you want your daughter to live with this kind of pain, yes?"

David: "I'm not sure."

Mark: "I think that you've lived with this driving, guilty pain all of your life and I think that that has been very hard for you and you've dumped this on your daughter."

David: "Perhaps..."

And then I say to the daughter, sitting in the chair opposite me: "Can you feel the lie that is sitting inside of your body and in your mind as a result of believing what your father told you? I want you to really feel it, take a bit of time to notice that you've been living with the lie inside of you and it's giving you indigestion and it's killing your spirit."

And I wait a while until I can see she's not just thinking about it but really *feeling* it. This is really important. It's really easy to *understand this* with the mind, but the important thing is to get it in the body and then you can begin to let go of it in the body.

So when I see that she's got it in her body, I then say to her: "Can you dissolve this lie in love? Can you let go of it?" (See 'Part 2 – Strategies, to learn to do this.)

She started to do this work and she has to do it more than once, because the lie has welded itself to her psyche and body and it has been there for years.

The above strategy is the most powerful one I know of to dissolve ignorance and Cultivate Wisdom.

So here's a short list of just some of the rules that create indigestion, anxiety and guilt in us.

- I must protect others from pain.
- Don't disappoint others.
- Keep others happy.

- I must be perfect – we're never quite sure how to, though.

- You have to study to be a "someone".

- You have to *be* a "someone".

- You have to be driven and ambitious.

- "Don't you dare talk back to me, contradict me, think you know it all … or you will be punished!"

- Be a lady/man/feminine.

- You have to be #1!

- Don't let your guests see your house in a mess.

- Don't let people see the holes in your socks/underwear.

- Don't let people see your imperfections.

- Don't let people know how much junk food you eat or how many Jerry Springer or Kardashian shows you watch.

- Don't show your ignorance around a million different things, i.e. pretend that you know everything. (There is the most immense freedom in being able to say "I have no idea what that word means" or "I didn't know that fact or understand what you are saying".) i.e. Be prepared to be ignorant and look stupid.

- Don't change your mind. We change our minds all the time. To say this is not okay or to deny it is to create insanity within.

- Don't be late or early – don't upset people!!!

- Be well-prepared and articulate.

- Don't watch too much TV.

- Don't sleep in the afternoons, except on a Sunday!

- Don't let the sun catch you in bed.

- Don't eat junk food.
- Don't change your mind.
- Finish what you start!
- Be well-prepared and articulate.
- I'm bad if I fail.
- Showing emotion is weakness.
- Don't be lazy.
- I musn't get judged or ridiculed.
- Be respectful and nice to everybody.
- I'm not clever enough, or thin enough, or rich enough, or successful enough, or attractive enough...

Learn to love yourself in spite of society's reasons not to – i.e. break the above rules when it's appropriate for you. I have seen many rich, thin, attractive, successful people who still feel that something is missing. And it is! What's missing is love for themselves – Original Self-Esteem.

"I'm not perfect – oh my God – you might find out!"

So, others might persecute us for not being perfect, but we persecute ourselves endlessly for this.

What is also fascinating is that we try to control our partners by stopping them from doing the things that freak us out – i.e. all of the above – and this destroys relationships.

EXAMPLE

A client of mine has a husband who continually tries to control her in an autocratic manner. "It's too cold in here," he says and turns on the aircon. "My mother's coming for lunch on Sunday," he tells her, without asking.

She gets extremely angry with him and tells me that he *"Has no right to do this!"*

Here is my dialogue with her:

Mark: "Are you sure that you are correct that he doesn't have a right to do this?"

Client: "Yes."

Mark: "And believing this makes you very angry, yes? And the more angry you get the more you believe you are right?"

Client: "Yes!"

Mark: "So let's check, what makes you so sure that you are right? Are you not being as autocratic as him deciding what rights he has and what rights he doesn't have?"

Client: (sheepishly) "Yes, I suppose so."

Mark: "If you didn't think you were right would you be less angry?"

Client: (laughing) "Yes."

Mark: "I'm thinking that believing you are right makes you angry and getting angry makes you believe more and more that you are right. If you stopped believing that you were right and you started to manage him and your anger better, you would be loving yourself more and he would feel more loved by you perhaps, in the long run, yes?"

And the point here is that people pronounce angrily to each other, without boundaries, that other people should and shouldn't be behaving in certain ways, but they're not giving themselves the freedom to respond in a boundaried, powerful way to deal with the behaviour that is a problem for them. This is deeply disempowering.

So the client above could simply say to him: "I'd prefer it if she didn't come for lunch on Sunday," without the long story of rules about what he should or shouldn't do.

CHECK EVERY ANXIETY ... EVERY GUILT

*The method to find what beliefs are running you
is to ask the question: What belief is behind the
anxiety and guilt I am feeling right now?*

I must emphasise that in the examples below, *you would need to do the emotional work in conjunction with dissolving the conditioning with the freeing belief.* (See Part 2 – Strategies – Activating love and power). Otherwise, you would just be doing affirmations, and this goes much deeper than doing an affirmation, much, much deeper.

Examples:

- "I'm scared of someone catching me unawares, unprepared."
  Belief: "I must be in control of what people see in me." Or "I must hide my inner world from the outer world."
  Freeing belief: "Nothing to hide, nothing to defend."

- "I'm scared that they will judge me and so I have to justify myself."

Belief: "I need to explain and defend my imperfections to the world."
Freeing belief: "I love my imperfections, they are for all to see."

- "I'm scared of failing."
Belief: "I'm only lovable if I succeed" or "I need to get love from someone else." "I must remain terrified of failure!"
Freeing belief: "Failing is a relative concept. I embrace all experiences."

- "I procrastinate and don't finish things."
Belief: "I'm a bad person if I leave things unfinished."
Freeing belief: "I finish some things, I don't finish others ... I am what I am, I do what I do." Or "I exit if something is wrong for me and I persist if it's right for me." "It just didn't work out. I move on."

- "I said or did something that upset someone."
Belief: "I'm a bad person if I upset someone" or "I shouldn't be selfish."
Freeing belief: "My intention is not to upset people, but it is inevitable that I will upset them."

DISSOLVING CONDITIONING IN THE PAST

One of the most beautiful ways to work with how conditioning gets imprinted into us is to go back to situations where we learned this nonsense from others. This process can save months and months of psychotherapy where people just sit in the feelings of pain in the past, or they interpret them or try to understand them.

Let me give you an example where I worked with this process with a client. This is a woman who is 40 years old. She has a senior management position, is tall and thin and attractive and has all of the external qualities that most women would want, yet essentially she believes that she is not good enough.

So I asked how she learned this and she says there are many instances but says that essentially she would be compared to her brother and told that she is not as smart as him or as polite as him or as kind as him.

I want you to picture a situation in which this kind of comparison was happening in your life and you can work on yourself in the way that I worked with her.

Here is my dialogue with her:

Mark: "So the message that you got from your mother in that moment was that your brother was good and you were bad because you were not as kind as your brother, yes?"

Client: "Yes that's right. I'm a bad person."

Mark: "So now I want to ask you, picturing yourself in the situation in the present, is she speaking the truth?"

Client: "Yes and it feels terrible and painful and awful."

Mark: "What do you think is behind your mother's belief that you are bad because you're not as kind as your brother?"

Client: "I suppose she's trying to make me a better person."

Mark: "And why do you think she's doing that?"

Client: "Maybe she thinks that I will chase people away and I will be isolated and won't have enough friends?"

Mark: "Ah! So she's frightened, yes, and trying to manipulate you? She is scared and is filled with anxiety about your future and how well it will work out?"

This is the primary basis of conditioning – fear and control!

Client: "Yes!"

Mark: "So she's not saying this for you, but because *she* is anxious, yes?"

Client: "Yes."

Mark: "So now I want you to just feel what it's like to notice that this is not the truth and it's not *for* you. It's for her ... Can you feel the lie that you are being fed. Just stop for a moment and notice what it feels like to no longer believe this lie...

(We pause for a moment here and she becomes tearful and she says that she has a sense of relief as she's beginning to realise that this is absolute nonsense that it's been injected into her.)

Mark: "Can you begin to feel that there is a love inside of you, that you are beautiful and perfect as you are and that love and power are your true nature and because you were a little girl you simply believed the nonsense that your mother fed you?"

Client: "Yes, just a little bit, it's beginning to happen."

And I get her to rest in this space, to spend a little more time there and then I do some *reciprocal switching*, getting her to go back to believing her mother that she is pathetic and awful and not good enough and then to move back into the sense of beautiful and magnificent and powerful and loving and then back to not okay and then back to okay and this is what one needs to do to begin to shift the energy from believing the conditioned garbage that is fed into us, into self-love.

And this is her homework.

Critical to this work is to see that much of our conditioning is for the "conditioner", not for us!

The fear of failure is such a strong factor in Acquired Self-Esteem that you might want to do the same thing regarding failure, as I have done in the above example. Our performance anxiety and fears of failure are created in just this way.

Notice anxieties and "guilts" as they come up in your life and check what belief is running behind them. Ask if it's true. See the fear and the desire to manipulate in the person who fed you the belief. Do *reciprocal switching* and come into your centre as much as possible.

A CAUTIONARY NOTE

Our conditioning runs deep, very deep. It is unlikely that you will dissolve all of it in one or two sessions. It usually takes somewhat longer.

I worked with a man who felt he was too harsh with people, unkind and cruel. I stressed with him that he needed to love himself before he softened this harshness, because if he didn't love himself now, when the harshness was transformed, he would find another reason not to love himself. If appreciating yourself is conditional, you will never rest in it fully.

FURTHER EXPERIENCES WITH CLIENTS

One of the most predominant beliefs in our culture is that you musn't tell people what you earn. Here is my dialogue with a client:

Mark: "So you don't tell people how much you earn?"

Client: "No."

Mark: "Why not?"

Client: "It's private."

Mark: "Why is it private?"

Client: "I don't know."

Mark: "Are you happy to go on believing something that has no reasoning behind it?"

And the client goes into silence ... they can see their own craziness.

And we live this craziness, repeatedly, for a lifetime!

Further discussion reveals that the client fears looking inferior – "I don't earn enough" – vs superior – "I earn more than you and don't want to look arrogant."

So the *primary belief* that underlies "Don't tell people how much you earn" is really an attempt to *manipulate* the other person's perception of you based on a fear of looking inferior or superior.

The parents who taught us this would have been more honest if they'd said: "I don't want you to look inferior or superior, so don't tell people how much you earn or ask them how much they earn."

There is no truth here, just a hidden agenda.

I think that this is a devastating fact. We manipulate our children as they grow up by telling them things that are blatantly untrue and which are designed to control their behaviour.

And these beliefs then control them as adults.

And people are worried about the Government - Big Brother?!

You might ask, what is our culture is about?

I think it is beliefs, masquerading as truth, designed to manipulate and control someone else's perceptions and behaviours.

And one of the most important issues underlying the lies we've been taught is: "It isn't money that makes the world go around, it's fear." Our parents and leaders are terrified!

In other words, we are trained to believe things because the person training us is frightened for us and of us and they then dump their fears on us.

You don't have to continue believing them.

The following are questions that I get clients to ask themselves in order to *Cultivate Wisdom:*

• Who told me this?

• What was their hidden agenda, if any, in telling me this? Did they have my best interests at heart, or was it for them – about their anxiety and need to control me?

• Or were they simply just frightened for me, i.e. not loving me?

• Was this a wise person who taught you this belief and if they were wise, perhaps this was a moment of ignorance for them?

• If it was about their anxiety, what were they frightened of? For example: "You are a good person if you do your homework."

You aren't "good" if you do your homework; you're just surviving within the system. Your parents are just frightened that you won't survive within the system. And I'm not saying that you don't need to survive within the system, but your parents don't tell you about the fear that underlies the issue. So it's not true that you're a good person if you do your homework, it just means you're fitting in with and surviving the system.

Finland has the best results from the school system of any country in the world and they've abolished homework. Kids spend four to five hours at school per day! They're allowed to behave as children. They're not miniature adults in training.

FREEZING IS WEAK!

I am working with a client, a young man of 30, recently promoted to financial director and feeling very anxious about his ability in this new position. He knows he needs Self-Esteem to work.

We start to work on his core pain. One of the examples from his list is around a speech he gave when in high school, where he froze completely. The dissolving work is going well and he tells me that about 80% of the pain is dissolved.

I have a hunch.

I ask him if there is a belief system which is inhibiting the dissolution of the last 20%.

He says: "Yes, there is. I believe that it is weak to freeze when speaking in front of people."

How can he dissolve the pain if he thinks that he should be in pain!

He considers the judgement "weak" to be the truth?

I ask him where this judgement came from and he says, "I don't know."

I then ask him: "Are you thinking that you were born with this and that as an infant this truth was simply there inside of you?"

Now he is uncertain. He doesn't know what to say. He's completely lost for words. And that is what the prison of our conditioned mind is like. It so often has no understanding of how a belief got to be there. We are in a prison and we have no idea who or what put us there, how we got there.

My client was brainwashed with this belief, which means it was inserted into his mind unconsciously. Here is the rest of dialogue that occurred between us:

Mark: "The question is, is this belief that you are weak if you freeze when giving a speech true?"

Client: "Yes."

Mark: "How did you decide whether this was true or not?"

Client: "I'm not sure, I've always just believed it." (And this is a really intelligent man – and he is not unusual!)

Mark: "So it wasn't a decision, it's just something you believed automatically, without question, yes?"

Client: "I suppose so."

Mark: "So you've been living with an unexamined belief for most of your life, yes? Is that wise, is that skilful?"

Client: "I guess not." Smiling...

Mark: "Why do you think this belief might be untrue?"

Client: "I'm not sure, it just seems to be a fact, I've always believed it..."

Very few people can at this point dismantle their own conditioning. They have absolutely no reference point for doing so. And so I have to help them, guide them out and this prison. Here is what I said to him.

Mark: "How do we work out what is strength and what is weakness? Can you think about the best leader you know in your career? Did they ever show vulnerability? Were they always infallible, perfect in every way? Can you notice that perhaps the people you've admired the most are those who are real, authentic, imperfect and fallible?

"Can you see that the people and the culture that taught you that mistakes and fallibility are weakness, were frightened of their own mistakes, but they were judging their own mistakes and scared of revealing them to the world. The fear of revealing these mistakes to the world makes them fragile and angry and controlling. Can you see that if you're always frightened of making a mistake that it makes you immensely vulnerable, in fact paranoid about 'screwing up'?

"And that if you see strength as being able to screw up and being able to be transparent about it, you are stepping into your power, because now you no longer live in fear of screwing up and of being criticised for it?"

And he responds with a knowing, insightful smile.

This is the start of his journey into dismantling the belief. If he keeps working at it, it can dissolve completely.

PROFESSIONALISM VERSUS INFORMALITY

I have been a management consultant for the last 17 years and one of the biggest things I have learned is that when it comes to the polarity of professional versus informal there is the most incredible lop-sidedness towards professionalism in managers and in staff.

The qualities of professional and informal are double-sided: they have benefits and drawbacks. Professionalism has wonderful qualities. It is reliable, organised, accountable, efficient, and presents a good image. The problem is that its downsides are immense. It can come across as heartless, cold, distant, uncaring and disconnected.

Informality has many drawbacks. It can be too casual, disconnected, uncaring and disengaged. The benefits are the opposite of the downsides of professionalism. It is caring, heartfelt, connected and engaged.

Because business was derived from the rather stiff British culture of the 19th century, it would seem that professionalism has been favoured in organisations. American culture and particularly the Dot Com Boom of the late 1990s has helped to change this.

What I'm talking about here is conditioning.

The conditioning towards professionalism has created a stiffness and a contraction and a disempowered-ness in the majority of people that I meet, both in and outside of business.

I will be talking in more detail later on about contraction and expansion as our energetic signature, our mental and emotional tone as it is reflected in our being. What I want to say here is that few people are aware of the degree to which they are living over-professionally and are too contracted in their interactions with the world.

Let me illustrate with a very simple example.

You're walking down the street and you see a neighbour whom you haven't met formally.

How do you greet them?

With a warm, open and relaxed smile?

Probably not.

Most people have a tense, half smile on their face. The greeting is tentative, waiting for rejection or acceptance.

There is immense anxiety in most people waiting to see if the other person will express warmth in *their* greeting *first!*

This is Acquired Self-Esteem, which creates a contracted professional exterior that disguises the fear of rejection. If you question people, they will usually admit to this, but they've never really thought about the fact that they've been conditioned to be like this based on their fear and their training in the culture.

Cultivating Wisdom is to see this contraction and the conditioning behind it and to begin to relax and expand into an openness and warmth that is not "paranoically" waiting to be discounted and undermined.

In the business context, this professionalism is reflected in the body language, the tone of voice and, most importantly, in the words that people use when talking to each other.

When managers deliver bad news to their staff, it's usually done in a stiff and tight way, with words such as: "Value add, strategic imperative, bottom line, the way forward, etc."

Simply changing your language and beginning to soften your facial expressions and to slow down can begin to dissolve this conditioning.

In essence, the socialisation process teaches us to contract and to live in fear, to protect ourselves, *and we think that this is the right and only way to be.*

One of the things that underlies this is that we've been trained to be accepted and to do well. Again, we're trained into Acquired Self-Esteem. Fear has been inserted into us and we remain trapped there and create a whole bunch of beliefs to support this.

Have you ever noticed how couples will try to control each other's behaviour socially? We don't want our partner to tell the truth about who they really are, how they really feel, what they really want.

I was trained by my parents to believe that asking for second helpings was rude. So having a good appetite or being very hungry was a bad thing – there was a judgement around this for me. I was also told that I have to finish all the food on my plate, that it was rude to my host to not finish my food.

So I should compromise *my* digestive system to please someone else!

A GAY MAN

Another client of mine, a 40-year-old gay man who had never had an intimate relationship and had not come out of the closet, had an immense sense of loneliness and depression as a result of this.

He had so much blocked and repressed pain that, in our first session, all I did was get him to feel and visualise the wall that was protecting him from the pain.

He had obviously never done this – very few people do this. We are such a "fix-it culture", always wanting to change and manoeuvre and reorganise and fix something. And what this often does is calcify and solidify the pain that is inside of us. But we don't know what else to do, so we continue to try to manipulate the pain and it is an endless, futile process.

So I spent an hour and a half just getting him to be with the pain and with the wall against the pain, protecting him against the pain.

And he watched the wall get bigger and smaller and change shape and the pain grow and shrink and grow and shrink. It was very difficult for him to do this because it was completely new. He was working in an entirely new process, in a foreign landscape.

But he did it, and at the end of an hour and a half he realised that his attempts to get rid of the wall, his defence against the pain, by resenting it and wishing he could get rid of it, were pointless.

At our next session we worked again for a short while with the wall and with his loneliness and then we got stuck. And so I asked him: "When did you get the feeling that being gay was unacceptable." And he replied that it was when he left school when he was 18. And I asked him how he felt at this time and he said: "I felt completely worthless and unacceptable."

Now I introduced the *Cultivating Wisdom* process. (What is really important here is that it was critical for us to do some of the emotional work first. Doing so enabled the *Cultivating Wisdom* technique to work with much more power and intensity.)

And so I asked the simple questions: "Was it the truth that being gay made you worthless? Were these people who taught you this, right? Are you sure that you were unacceptable because you were gay?

"Can you see that when society told you that you are bad because you are gay you were treating them as though they were the world's top scientists who were speaking the truth?

"Can you feel how you gave your power away when you treated them as though they were scientists speaking the truth? Can you reclaim your power and stop believing them in your *mind* and in your *body*?"

And for the first time in his life he began to question the assumption that he had lived with for over two decades.

And slowly, slowly, as we discussed this, his sense of worthlessness dissolved and he began to believe that being gay could mean that he was lovable.

This is so fascinating, because as we did the work and dismantled the bars of this prison of conditioning, he said to me: "My body is feeling bigger and broader and stronger." And I allowed him to simply have that experience and to enjoy it and feel his power and his transformation truly began to flower.

Cultivating Wisdom is to dissect and dis-assemble the garbage we have ingested from our parents and our culture *and ourselves*. There is great freedom in letting go of this garbage.

Cultivating Wisdom is what you want to learn to do whenever you are dissolving an emotion and you hit a dead end and at other times too, to deepen the dissolving process.

Cultivating Wisdom is a process whereby questions are used to challenge the assumptions of the mind to ensure that the beliefs held in the mind are not an obstruction to healing, growth and transformation.

I am endlessly astonished both at the power of our belief systems and the extent to which our spontaneous creativity *and healing* is blocked by them.

> *"Whether we believe something to be true or not determines a vast proportion of our present and future experience."*

Now I would like to use an analogy to illustrate why this issue of truth is so important.

If a dishevelled-looking old man stands on the street corner with a sandwich board saying "The end of the world is nigh", you will laugh at him and his sandwich board. You won't believe him for a second.

If six of the most famous scientists in the world appear on CNN saying that a comet is going to crash into the planet tomorrow and destroy us, you are going to believe them.

And you will most likely get a very, very anxious and start making plans as to what you going to do about it to manage the situation.[2]

It is very interesting to notice how we love to think that our thoughts are true. It makes us feel good, it makes us feel self-righteous and powerful. So you might want to let go of your arrogant excitement about the fact that you believe certain thoughts to be true *and question them!*

In working with thousands of people over many years, I realise that the people who want to grow the most are those who are prepared the question their thoughts.

People who want to grow the least tend to be very rigid in their belief systems and not open to the possibility that their belief systems are untrue.

What I found is that people either have no answer to these questions or, at best, their answers are very superficial. Some of the beliefs we have are self-created, and the most difficult ones to dislodge are often the ones which appear to be very true.

SUICIDE AND CONDITIONING

I was working with a couple. The husband's parents had moved into a cottage on their property.

The mother-in-law was experiencing senile dementia and the father-in-law was drinking excessively. Both were in the late 70s.

---

2 I had a really amusing experience with a client on one occasion. She came from a fundamentalist religious background. I gave her the analogy of the CNN scientists and the sandwich board guy and she immediately stopped me, saying: "I wouldn't believe the scientists, because I know what my bible says!" I was stunned for a moment and then simply moved on to something else. The power of a belief system is sometimes beyond all reason!

There was conflict between the couple around the father-in-law's drinking and the concern was that he would kill himself with the excess of alcohol.

The wife had the greatest anxiety about the father-in-law killing himself.

I said to her: "Is it such a terrible thing if he kills himself?" She was visibly shocked at my question. People are usually shocked if you question a very deep-seated and *unquestioned* cultural belief.

And she replied, "Yes", looking visibly horrified.

And so I asked if she was sure about this and she said yes, but I kept repeating the question, trying to establish if she was absolutely sure that it was a terrible thing if this old, miserable man killed himself. Eventually she said to me: "Well I don't know. I've always thought that suicide has to be a bad thing. I've never really questioned it."

Precisely!

There is tremendous power in questioning *everything* we have been taught.

I then proceeded to share my views around suicide. Our culture believes that suicide is terrible, that it's always bad. I have worked for years with clients who have wanted to kill themselves – just two of them tried and failed. Many of these clients had loved ones who had killed themselves and honestly, sometimes it often feels to me like a truly understandable act on behalf of the person committing it.

Why?

Because they're so utterly miserable that they need to find a way out of the misery of their lives.

The idea that "God never gives you something you can't handle" is preposterous. I think people believe it because they have been conditioned to do so. How does this explain the one million people a year who kill themselves? They couldn't handle their lives, so they ended it!!!

I know of one woman who killed herself because she had the most horrendous tinnitus for a number of years that drove her completely insane. She tried everything medically known to deal with it but nothing worked.

It seems to me that suicide was her only sane option.

I worked with another woman of about 60 whose husband committed suicide after 35 years of marriage. (My strategy here is attributable to Dr Demartini).

Initially she talked about the misery and pain of him having hanged himself and how sad she was and how desperate she was about what he did. And so I started to ask some questions along the lines of "Were you happily married?"

"Oh no, she said."

And she proceeded to describe the horrors of living with him.

After she had listed all of his negative qualities, which included excessive drinking, emotional and physical abuse, raping her, having conflictual relationships with the entire family, his emotional distance etc, I said to her: "So you miss these things a lot?"

And she laughed and said: "No of course not."

So I said to her: "If you think about all of the things that he's done to you and the way he's behaved – and I went through the list again – are you still thinking that his suicide was a terrible thing?"

And she said to me, leaning forward, as though someone else might hear her, and said, in a surreptitious whisper: "No, but don't tell anyone in my church group, please."

The church group issue is really wonderful. She doesn't want me to tell her group because the conditioning around suicide is so powerful and her group contains and needs to hold onto this conditioning – it's one of the rules of the group – so to tell the group would be to threaten the group or to have them threaten her.

I would think first the former and then the latter!

We discussed this a little further and I helped her to see that her missing him was really based on a belief system into which she was conditioned, which said that she had to feel terrible that he had committed suicide and was now dead when, in fact, she was inwardly delighted.

This experience got me thinking that if I ever wrote a book about suicide it would be titled *Suicide, the Secret Celebration*.

People who have been depressed for many years and finally commit suicide leave behind them loved ones who are relieved of the immense burden of living with that depression for all that time.

It has to be a celebration for them!

But they're not allowed to celebrate because our culture says suicide is always a terrible thing.

Now I know that you might be horrified by what I've been saying.

And all I can say is, that's probably because you've never questioned this belief *and* it is also probably very deep-seated.

And please note there are many instances when suicide is desperately

> *painful for those that are left behind,*
> *particularly in the case of children.*
> *What I've been talking about here are the instances*
> *when the blessings*
> *of the suicide far outweigh the pain.*

I mentioned earlier that we try to manipulate others with conditioned beliefs masquerading as truth. Can you see that what is hidden beneath the lie that suicide is bad is our discomfort with suicide? It is our repressed anxiety and threat and horror at suicide that leads us to say: "It is bad!"

Have you ever felt guilty at your own suicidal thoughts?

What is really important to understand about this conditioning is that I do understand that conditioning needs to happen:

> *But it could be done more skilfully!*

It is the **way** in which we are conditioned that is the problem, not the fact that we are conditioned.

Let me illustrate. We are taught that lying is bad. But everyone lies, so the parent who tells their child "Don't you dare lie to me" is being immensely unskilful and destructive toward their child.

So what would be far more skilful would be to say to a child:

"I would prefer it if you told the truth more of the time and certainly it is a much better way to live, to tell the truth as much of the time as possible, but lying is unavoidable. So let's start an ongoing discussion around lies and the truth and discuss why we need to lie at times, what causes us to do it and how to overcome the need to tell lies and to learn to honour ourselves when we do need to lie!"

My investigation of this tells me that lying has immense advantages.

Let me give you a short list:

It gives us freedom to do what we like, it gives us privacy and helps us to avoid conflict. It is a deeply protective mechanism and it helps us to manipulate others to get what we want.

Pretty good, huh?

MORE EXAMPLES

I want to give some further detailed examples of the kinds of beliefs we ingest as kids and go on believing for the rest of our lives:

"Never give up what you have started."

This is one of the most destructive beliefs I have seen in my clients over the years. What is so fascinating is that not one of the people that I've seen who believe this has questioned this belief.

Which means that they stay in relationships and in careers and in projects to which they are just not suited. This causes untold agony for them. Doing something that is not right for you is painful and to keep doing it for long periods of time is going to be depressing. It's not aligned with your original nature and so it will not support the development and the maintenance of Original Self-Esteem.

It is mostly our parents who teach us this. Parents who come from a Calvinistic background.

And you don't have to be a Calvinist to have this belief. My parents gave it to me and they were Jewish!

The first thing I say to these people when they have this belief system is: "Have you heard of Stephen Covey's book, *The 7 Habits of Highly Effective People*?" And many of them say yes, and then I say: "Do you know the habit, 'Know when to exit?'" If they do. I ask them what they think it means.

If they can't remember, or don't know it, I explain.

It means that people with great Self-Esteem know when they're doing the wrong thing, or when they are in the wrong relationship or in the wrong team or in the wrong business or in the wrong friendship.

And they leave ... fast.

They don't ruminate endlessly about why they should stay there and why they shouldn't hurt somebody else by leaving. Or how guilty they will feel when the other person is hurt.

They do what is aligned with their beliefs and their values at that point in time and they exit.

The big mistake with the belief that one should stick to what one is doing is that it's not even a half-truth. It's really completely incorrect. So I have adjusted it to run as follows:

> *Don't give up what you've started if it's right for you and exit as quickly as possible if it's not.*

The "quickly as possible" part is really important. I have asked dozens of groups that I've worked with the following question: "How long have you stayed in a job or in a relationship longer than you should have?" And 80% of them put their hands up. The other 20% are wondering if they should own up or not!

Why do we stick around for too long? Because we have a conditioned belief system that says we can't leave, not because it's the right thing for us, but because it's a rule that we have ingested, which we think we should follow blindly. An ignorant commandment to which we are slaves.

And one of the things that rule is saying is that you will be a better person if you don't give up. And again it's: "I don't want you to be an inferior person who fails in life." So the fear of failure is again an underlying issue here.

Obviously there are also occasions when we don't leave, or dump someone, because we are plain and simply frightened – which means we need to get into our power to dissolve the fear!

To do something because you were told it is the truth is to reject yourself.

Self-rejection is a prison. Cultivating Wisdom is your escape plan.

"I shouldn't be having an affair with a married man/woman!"

Really? Approximately 60% of American men and 40% of women have affairs.

It's what people do.

It's reality.

"Shouldn't" is resisting and fighting reality.

It's the Victim position.

A much better question would be: how come am I having an affair?

What is happening in my marriage or inside me that is causing me to have the affair?

Do I want to work with it or not?

Am I having the affair because I am scared of getting out on my own and then looking for a fulfilling connection?

Do I need emotional affirmation or sex so badly that I have to have an affair to get it?

Can I have a discussion with my partner around affirmation and sex and start to work on it, rather than have an affair?

> *The judgement about having the affair is really a way of avoiding all of these very difficult and painful questions.*

These questions illustrate something really important about this process. They show us how simplistic our conditioned beliefs usually are. It is very easy to fall back on a simple injunction given to us by someone else and not examine it.

If you want to move into a place of wisdom and power, just start to question the assumptions handed down to you unquestioningly.

And I want to tell you, I have worked with some couples where the affair has transformed their marriage. It takes a lot of work and it's painful, but it's possible – though not common.

If it's not possible, learn the lessons and move on. I don't mean to sound glib here. Moving on can be extremely difficult, especially if there are kids involved.

And I really can't tell you if it's better for the kids to experience a bad marriage or experienced the pain of divorce. Some kids do a lot worse with divorce than others. Many kids say to their parents who have waited until the kids have grown up to get divorced: "Why didn't you get divorced sooner!?"

"I'm bad if I fail."

What does badness really mean?

What is failure?

Is failure a fact or judgement or both?

If it's a judgement, what is it based on?

Everything in our lives is endlessly both working well and failing, isn't it?

The entire world of matter is basically coming into creation and decaying into destruction.

If failure is just a fact – things fail and work and fail and work – then why do you have to add the judgement on top of it?

Did people simply teach you to judge yourself in order to control you?

Isn't this what your parents did?

I described earlier how babies, learning to walk, never consider the fact that they might be failing at it.

Failure is a learned concept. It can be unlearned.

PERFORMANCE ANXIETY

Performance anxiety is the scourge of First World culture.

When I created this book I just pictured myself as a six-year-old little boy eager and energised and excited and sitting in a school classroom and suddenly feeling like I was terrified of failing, of screwing up.

And so I visualised the mature Mark coming up to that little Mark and saying to him:

"It's okay, Markie. Can you begin to relax and just enjoy what you are doing and forget about performing well and the teacher criticising you and failing and feeling bad? Can you just feel the love in your heart and the joy and inspiration inside of you that you've always had all these years and dissolve

all the fear away so that you can feel magnificent and not get into what people call performance anxiety?"

As a therapist I use a technique called TRE: the stress and trauma release process created by Dr David Berceli.

It's a beautiful somatic process for releasing trauma in the body. The clients do some simple exercises, lie down on the floor on their backs, and the body begins to spontaneously tremor and release all the stress and trauma that is locked inside of it.

At the end of the first session I give them some notes describing how to do the exercises on their own. These exercises actually precede the tremor process and every single adult without fail expresses an anxiety that they won't be able to do it properly.

Why?

Because they've been conditioned to believe that they have to perform, they musn't screw up and they must avoid criticism and failure and judgement.

This is insanity!

It's not the truth, it's just conditioning, it's just a bunch of lies you've absorbed innocently and so you can dissolve them in the truth.

It's really fascinating how parents try to control their kids.

They are scared that you might fail at school or in your relationships. They think that you will be lonely and not succeed in life and they can't cope with this fear and so they get angry with you.

So, is their judgement the truth?

Are any judgements really the truth?

If you struggle in your business for years and feel like a failure because of it, is this the truth?

Are you really a failure?

What if your business starts to succeed and you feel like a success? Is this the truth?

And then your business fails for reasons beyond your control or maybe you're not sure of the reasons why your business failed. Does this make you suddenly a failure when you were previously a success?

I think not.

The judgements associated with the ups and downs of life are not the truth. They are just judgements, based on history, conditioning and culture.

They are simply movements of the mind, conditioned to rate and score and judge – endlessly!

First World culture places a huge premium on winning and doing well and succeeding, on making money and having power and being attractive. My mother used to say: "No one remembers the bridesmaid." The hidden lie was: "You have to win to be okay."

Third World cultures don't tend to do this, as far as I am aware.

Who says the First World values are correct? People's values differ; they aren't the truth. There isn't a gold standard for the correct and right values to have.

I have seen people make a great deal of money even when they're completely uninspired by what they're doing, which breaks all the rules associated with New Age ideas that say the energy you bring to a task is reflected in the outcome.

These issues are complex and we far too easily make decisions about ourselves and other people, which put us in the success box or the failure box.

When you see the lies underlying your conditioning, freedom beckons.

"Showing emotion, particularly if I am a man, is weakness."

Who got to decide that cowboys don't cry?

Probably cowboys!

How is manhood defined?

Women often say they don't like men who *can't* show emotion and yet women often, paradoxically, like men who are in control and don't show emotion, and this is called strength.

Emotions can leave us feeling out of control and chaotic, and many men and a fair proportion of women don't like this feeling, and so we judge something that we don't like and call it "weakness". It might be more accurate for a man to say I'm scared of my feelings and I feel out of control internally when I experience feelings, so I call it "weak" in order to try and escape the feelings of loss of control.

Weakness is just an arbitrary term designed to control myself and then designed to judge others and to control them too.

"I have addictions to junk food, chocolates, cigarettes, television, sex ... which makes me bad and I can't change any of this."

When we believe that these things are bad, we are essentially believing that we have control over our addictions and that we should be able to exercise this control. Are you sure that you actually do have control? If the cause of your addiction was due to some genetic or biological factor, outside of your control, would you think differently about this?

Twin study research has shown that up to 60% of addictions are due to genetic factors and, last time I looked, it wasn't that easy to control one's genetic inheritance.

The field of epigenetics is showing that genes can be altered, but how to do this and the mechanisms of this process are still in their infancy.

My experience is that generally speaking we can't control our thoughts.

How can you judge yourself for something over which you have no control?

People make judgements about their own and others' person-alities. If we have nocontrol over our personalities, then to judge them is criminal.

Not only this, but we think that our judgements are the truth. Truth is dependent on perspective, even at the most basic level. Up and down are relative. If you're out in space, there is no up and there is no down.

It looks like the sun goes round the Earth but it doesn't. It looks as if the sun comes up in the morning and goes down in the afternoon, but it doesn't. The Earth spins on its axis and so it looks like the sun comes up and down, but there isn't even an up and a down!

"I am lazy."

Everybody is lazy for what they are not interested in (with thanks to John Demartini for this insight). So I am lazy when it comes to doing my admin', which simply means that I'm not interested in admin.

I'm lazy when it comes to putting out the garbage or fixing the garage door or shopping or writing reports – *because they don't interest me.*

Everybody is organised and focused and disciplined and motivated for what they're interested in and everybody is lazy – unfocused, disinterested and unmotivated – in the areas that they have no interest.

According to the *Gallup Strengths Finder* work, I have the *activator* strength as number one on my list. I didn't choose this strength; I was born with it. So if I get an idea, I just jump to it. It's natural for me. If this strength is number 32 on your list, you are going to be called a procrastinator and you are going to be told that you are bad when you procrastinate or that you are lazy.

It's a lie!

So again the judgement of the word 'lazy' is simply there to control ourselves or somebody else. It's not the truth.

People are endlessly using judgements
and thinking that they are truth.
They have nothing to do with the truth; they're just judgements
and opinions, designed to control ourselves or somebody else.

"I have to be nice to everybody, or most people, or to family."

Why?

So that you can look good or create harmony. I think the origin of this belief is based on a fairly reasonable assumption that if we were to let our selfish and aggressive instincts run riot, then our society would dissolve into chaos.

The problem is, we then generalise this to all situations and we think we have to be nice *everywhere*. All that does is suppress our needs and wants and create internal repression and chaos because of it.

My experience of living is that we need to know when to be kind and when to be tough ... cruel. There are many people who will exploit your kindness.

Discriminate!

But our parents didn't teach us to discriminate.
They just taught us an oversimplified rule!

One of the major difficulties here is that if you are a rescuer, which is a person who tends to be too nice to people and to be kind inappropriately, then you are going to be addicted to harmony and avoidant of conflict. Becoming more powerful therefore has drawbacks, because it's going to destroy your addiction and face you with the things that you fear.

You need to do a lot of emotional work around this as well as work with your belief systems.

And indeed this applies to much of this work. Some people have a preference for working emotionally and some people have a preference for working intellectually. Most people need to work on both levels.

"I should be smarter than I am."

You're as smart as you are. And IQ doesn't change.

Why do you want to be smarter?

To impress people? To impress yourself?

To boost your ego?

So that you can be happier?

So that you can have a better job or career?

Now the last of these can perhaps be quite useful, but I know PhDs who are insecure about their intellect – having a PhD doesn't make them "feel good enough".

I had a client who worked with a Nobel laureate in genetics. Having a Nobel Prize is one of the most prestigious things you can have in our culture and yet this man had very low Self-Esteem. This was evidenced by the fact that when he met someone for the first time he couldn't wait to tell them that he had a Nobel Prize!

So again the issue of fantasies rears its head. You have a fantasy that if you had a better intellect, you would feel better about your life, but you won't, because even if your newfound intellectual prowess were to arise, your mind would find something else that was missing in your life, which is what the mind does, endlessly, incessantly.

"I should be more successful than I am."

Really!?

You think successful people don't have problems and issues and difficulties and areas of deflated Self-Esteem?

They also often rely too much on their success for their Self-Esteem so when the success isn't manifesting itself, they crash.

Many high performing people are in Original Self-Esteem when they are actually *doing* something. This is when they are in that flow state, not thinking about what they are doing, not being self-conscious about it. It is my belief that one of the characteristics of great sportspeople and business people is that they *recover faster* from bouts of Acquired Self-Esteem than most other people, rather than that they never go into it.

The problem for most of them is that when they are not performing and doing, they get as lost as the rest of us in their ruminative minds, doubting themselves and getting depressed.

"I must contribute to society or to charities or give to the needy or the sick."

There are two kinds of giving: authentic spontaneous giving and manipulative giving.

Much of the time our giving comes from the latter. It is ego driven. We want to look good by trying to manipulate others' perceptions of us or our perception of ourselves, so we give in order to feel like we are a "good person".

Most people are doing this much of the time, everywhere. It's not a bad thing; it's just human and it has great benefits for those we are giving to. However, often we don't want to give – it's not aligned with our authenticity. In the past I engaged myself in community work that I felt somewhat inspired by, but the projects didn't work out and so I let them go. Ultimately they didn't make me feel good.

I see people who just feel guilty because they are not giving enough to others. We give as much as we give, as a result of who we are. Perhaps you are not a Mother Theresa or an Albert Schweitzer. Does that make you a bad person?

"Our sexual relationship should remain consistently good and synchronised for 50 years."

This is one of my best.

It captures the insanity of the garbage with which we are indoctrinated quite beautifully. I would like to illustrate this by sharing some details about a client.

He is 40 years old, successful, good-looking but insecure and lacking in Self-Esteem in his intimate relationships. He is able to attract good-looking women but is always thinking that they may be leaving him soon. His partner gets very stressed at work and loses interest in sex when stressed and he starts to think that something is wrong with him, that something is wrong with the relationship.

Our culture subscribes to the belief that both parties should want sex at the same frequency for 50 years. So the first question is, is this true? Where did you get the idea that it is true?

And people usually have no idea where they got this idea, but most people believe it. People also think that their partner should be equally affectionate throughout the relationship. And our yardstick is the first three months of the relationship when we are infatuated, and infatuation, by definition, isn't reality and so it's impossible to be maintained.

> *I think God created infatuated "in-love" states as a trick*
> *to ensure the continuation of the species.*

And so my client says that while his partner is stressed and she's not being affectionate he starts to ruminate and have fantasies about whether she will leave and how much she really cares about him and so on.

And the fantasies are designed to control what is happening and they drive him insane. They are designed to reduce anxiety *but they increase his anxiety!*

He then says that if she does something that fuels his anxiety, such as being a little disconnected and not affectionate, he feels even worse. And why does this happen?

> *Because he is emotionally empty or in great pain.*

So now you might say: "But I'm not emotionally empty." And I would say the following:

Maybe 5% of parents are able to take care of their children's emotional needs.

When an infant is crying, very few parents are able to take care of the needs of the child's pain from a place that is solid and stable and balanced and loving and without anxiety or irritation or frustration.

Most of us are way too neurotic to be able to love the child in this way. What this means is that children's needs go unmet and as kids we create defences to protect ourselves from the pain of these unmet needs. Most people are not aware of the defences that they've created. They would tell you that there absolutely F.I.N.E. Unfortunately, they're kidding themselves – they're not fine. (F.I.N.E. means Freaked out, Insecure, Neurotic and Exhausted.)

A new term has been developed by clinicians called Developmental Trauma Disorder (DTD), which refers to the traumatic effects of parental neglect on the developing child's brain and body.

From this traumatised place our engagement with life comes from a protected place and we use drink and drugs and sex and TV and Facebook and food and sport and work to avoid this pain, to fill the emptiness.

And so this question "Does she still love me?" is asking the wrong question. It's looking outside of oneself for the answer, to solve the problem.

There is a wonderful story about a man who's lost his car keys at night in the street. The stranger passes by and offers to help. They're looking under the street lamp and it's very clear that the keys aren't there and so the stranger says to him, "Where did you lose the keys?" And the man replies, "Over there in the bush."

And with great surprise the stranger says, "So why are we looking here underneath the street lamp?" And he answers, "It's too dark in the bush!"

It's much easier to ask the question "Does she love me?" and then to engage in ruminations looking for proof to protect oneself against this anxiety.

> But it's the wrong question.
>
> The right question is: "Can I feel the emptiness or pain inside of me behind this question and dissolve it in power and love?"

"You must give me what I want!"

Most people behave in ways that suggest that the biggest problem in life is that other people don't give them what they want.

The problem is that we have thousands of "wants" every day. And the people we interact with have thousands of "wants" every day. It is utterly impossible for all of our wants to be perfectly synchronised, yes?

So let's take another very common example.

Women have much more perfectionistic attitudes around keeping house than men.

They are more focused than men around closing cupboard doors, putting out the rubbish, not leaving clothes lying around on the floor, having the dishes washed immediately at all times, changing light bulbs, having a dust-free house etc – you know the scenario.

So the wife attacks the husband for not adhering to the standards she has around house hygiene. He responds by attacking her back and defending himself vehemently.

I have seen couples fighting about this stuff for 50 years and more!

Couples get locked into cycles of fighting that are simply about my "wants" versus your "wants".

So I want to explore what's going on underneath the wanting.

The wife cannot tolerate cupboards being open and rubbish not put out. This causes her pain internally. She is not aware of the pain, which is the primary emotion; she is just aware of the anger, which is a secondary emotion.

And so she dumps the secondary emotion on her husband.

He is not particularly in touch with the pain of being attacked, which is again primary, and so attacks her back, which is, again, secondary.

If you are living in secondary emotions, you are going to struggle to resolve the primary problem.

This is life.

This is what people do for their entire lifetimes!

I'm working with a husband who's just had this kind of fight with his wife and he really wants to work on the issue, his issue. And he's taking notes as I discuss this, which is useful but it's not doing the work.

So I ask him to put aside his notepad and to picture his wife attacking him for not putting out the rubbish and closing the cupboards etc and to feel the hurt. And when he can feel the hurt, I ask him to bring in a sense of innocence – which I will be talking about later and which he does very well in the Self-Esteem work – to dissolve the hurt.

And he does this and his face completely transforms. From anxious, contracted and tight, to open and lose and expanded. So simple, and yet people don't know that this is what they need to do. Of course, he needs to do this dozens of times in order to really transform himself.

The next step is how to deal with his wife, i.e. how to manage the conversation strategically, skilfully. I will give a brief summary here but I will deal with this in more detail in the chapter on boundaries.

This is what I suggest he say to her once he has dissolved the hurt:

"Sweetie, I can see that this is really painful for you. Has it always been this way? Do I upset you in a whole lot of other ways around the house?" And now he gives her an opportunity to talk about her anger and pain around these issues.

And the next bit can only happen when she has calmed down, because if he says this next paragraph when she is still angry, *it won't work!*

And then he says to her: "You know, I can try and do these things better for you. The problem is it's not really my personality and it's gonna be very difficult for me to change my personality, yes? (smiling) And then you have a whole lot of things you want me to do differently and I have a whole lot of things I want you to do differently and it's impossible for us to change our personalities to completely suit each other, but I can make an effort for you and I will. And perhaps I could tell you about some of the things I would like to be different, yes?"

This is a respectful dialogue. About 4% of couples can do this. (I'm smiling...)

"Respect your elders and people in positions of authority and power."

Wisdom tells me that we need to give respect where it is earned, not because of credentials. Our culture teaches the opposite.

Doctors, surgeons, CEOs, heads of state, older people are supposed to be respected because of their position and status.

My partner, Sue, runs a very successful business, importing gas stoves from Italy. She also runs her store. People come into the store and assume that she is the shop assistant with no skills. They treat her with no respect. People phone in and because she is a woman she is very often asked if she can put them onto the manager.

She says that she is the owner of the business. Often they don't believe her, presumably because she is a woman.

The disrespect she is shown by customers on a daily basis is monumental, completely out of the ballpark.

I, on the other hand, am a clinical psychologist. This presumably means that I'm a person of stature and respect.

Absurd isn't it.

I am very rarely treated in anyway disrespectfully by my clients who, by definition, have significant emotional problems. So why the difference in treatment towards Sue and toward myself?

Am I more deserving of respect than Sue, who is an extraordinary woman, with amazing emotional intelligence, quite apart from her immense business skills?

Most profoundly not.

I think it's because people are trained in our culture to respect somebody's title and position rather than the person.

It's absurd.

Sue is a genius at what she does.

Why is she not as respected by her clients as I am?

Because the conditioning of the culture says it is not about the person; it's about their age, status or position.

This is insane.

But we don't question the insanity.

One of the consequences of this issue is that doctors and psychologists, among others, get far more respect than is their due, which means that people don't question them and challenge them and make them more accountable, to be ethical in their behaviour towards their clients.

It also means that the clients and patients are disempowered. If you respect a title rather than the person for what they are, you have no power.

It is very common nowadays to criticise the medical profession for abuses of clients, but giving respect to a title is to be without power and it asks to be disrespected.

So this is a very big issue around personal power.

To give respect where it is not due is not good for your Self-Esteem and hence it is not good for your health at all levels.

So, what do all these beliefs I have been talking about have in common?

They're judgements. They are "oughts" and "shoulds" and "musts" and "have to's" and "got to's".

You can bet that just about every single "should" we have is not truth. How can it be? It's an idea designed to control somebody else or oneself, and control almost always comes out of fear or the need to win and feel safe.

It's not easy for truth to come out of a need to control.

The need to control is desperate, contracted, divided and divisive.

Saying that a judgement is the truth is designed to give it power. We hope that if we call a judgement truth, we will have greater influence over others and ourselves and sometimes it does, sometimes it works.

If it never worked we would probably stop doing it.

Just because it works doesn't mean it's the truth.

It's just a manipulation that worked.

And as long as we are functioning for such a large part of the time from our egos, then we are going to be manipulative.

For decades I lived believing that manipulation was bad and that we shouldn't do it. I derived this belief system from my left-wing lecturers and colleagues at university who were really addicted to their "philosophies" as being the truth.

Just in case you suffer from this malady yourself, let me ask you this:

If you wanted to suggest to your intimate partner a very expensive holiday destination when you knew that neither of you really had the funds to support it, would you bring up the holiday topic on a Friday afternoon just after they had arrived home incredibly stressed out from a really tough week?

No, you'd wait until Sunday morning over breakfast when they're relaxed and happy.

That's a manipulation. So is your job interview. So is your first date!

Do you behave the same way with your partner now as you did on your first date?

How about meeting your in-laws for the first time, or talking to your CEO...

Regarding the latter, just think about how you talk to your colleagues vs your CEO. Is your tone, attitude etc the same as talking to a colleague?

I could go on endlessly giving you examples to illustrate this point, but the above examples should, I hope, be enough.

Manipulation is part of life.

My final point is that when I am manipulating, if it's for the good of both of us, it's benign; if it's only for my own good, then it's malignant. I prefer to spend most of my time in the former position.

Cultivating Wisdom requires that you look at the belief system that keeps you stuck in your pain. So if you've done something to hurt someone else and you feel guilty, what may prevent you from dissolving the guilt is the belief that you truly are bad. As long as you believe you are truly bad, no psychological process is going to change your ability to dissolve the pain.

Whenever you get stuck on dissolving a painful issue, check the beliefs and watch what happens.

A FINAL NOTE

A word of caution. Don't be in too much of a rush to blame your parents or society for all the lies that have been conditioned into you, for the straitjacket, this prison that you live in, because we also lie to ourselves.

Every time you have a fantasy about the next best thing that is going to happen – your new smart phone upgrade, the World Cup finals that your team is competing in on this weekend, the fabulous holiday to the Caribbean, your wedding, or this supposedly perfect person that you have just met that seems perfect because of your "in love" state – you are creating a fantasy, and a fantasy isn't reality, it's a lie.

And most of the time the consequence of lying to ourselves is that we get depressed.

It's called pro-depressant thinking – i.e. thinking that causes depression.

And really finally – the biggest lie of all:

I should get what I want.

And then super-finally, the biggest rule:

Don't break the rules.

Which means that the greatest service you can do yourself is to know which rules to break and to learn to love yourself when you break them.

When you no longer are living the lies given to you as truth, you are free to be your authentic, spirited self, loving yourself in spite of others' reasons not to.

Go to chapter 20 for a summary of the section.

CHAPTER 7

BOUNDARIES

They want you to kneel before them
And you do - for fear is your master.
And you give them your Spirit, your Soul,
To straighten your spine in love and power
Is to suffer the slings and arrows of disrepute.

Guilt and shame are your partners all of the days
Of your life,
As long as you need love,
Fear hurting them,
More than you will love yourself.
So is this life sentence written in the sky
Only undone with great and unremitting courage.

And rising from your knees, you reach upwards
Your heart beating with the very power of mother earth
All subjugation gone
Your power uncoiled,
Unfurled, your flag of honour of Self.

To speak and act and live from the truth that is You,
Is noble and wise and gratifying
To the heart of your Soul.

Mark Peter Kahn.

"Power enables boundaries."

Boundaries are critical to building power.

Boundaries are vital to survival.

Boundaries are a crucial indicator of self-love, Self-Esteem.

Why?

Because the world is filled with people and situations that are just waiting to overpower you, and no boundary ... equals no power.

"If you are disempowered, you will invite someone in to
overpower you."
Dr John F. Demartini

Dr Demartini is right.

I have watched this in others and in myself thousands of times.

As I have mentioned, when I left school I had no idea who I was, what I wanted from life or where I was going. I was almost as disempowered as anyone could get.

I was depressed, anxious, paranoid and I had very little self-worth.

Unwittingly I was inviting my parents in to overpower me and overpower me they did, by marching me off to the University of the Witwatersrand to do a B.Com degree.

I didn't want to do a B.Com. I didn't have any sense of an 'I' really.

It was hell personified.

The Great Hall – which is where all of the major university productions and presentations and ceremonies were held – was this Greek-looking building with vast pillars and perhaps eight or 10 big columns holding up the roof at the entrance.

I remember walking down the steps – there must have been 50 of them – leading onto a piazza and not feeling that I could walk properly because people must be watching me. How's that for paranoia and being disempowered!?

How could I have been anything but depressed?

I managed to finish the B. Com, heaven knows how, given that I'm still not sure of the difference between a debit and credit ... and I was still disempowered.

So my parents stepped in again and marched me off to a friend of theirs who owned that margarine factory I talked about previously.

Just notice in your own life how, when you are unsure of yourself, someone will step in and be certain for you, overpower you.

If you hate conflict, that means you're disempowered in this arena, and don't be surprised when you feel bullied and pushed around.

If you don't like talking about money or asking for money owed to you, expect people to take you for a ride in this arena.

The greatest, most magnificent line about boundaries comes from the movie, *The Girl with the Dragon Tattoo.*

There is the psychopath in the movie and the hero is checking out his home, walking around outside and the psychopath comes home. He invites him in for a drink. The hero knows that this is dangerous but his need to be polite, his lack of boundary, causes him to say yes.

Once inside, the psychopath takes him into his basement, ties him to a chair and begins to torture him. The psychopath then says:

"Let me ask you something? Why don't people trust their instincts? They sense something is wrong ... You knew something was wrong, but you came back into the house. Did I force you, did I drag you in? No. All I had to do was offer you a drink. It's hard to believe that the fear of offending can be stronger than the fear of pain. But you know what? It is.

The fear of offending someone is your greatest limitation to creating a boundary.

Your fear of looking mean and nasty and arrogant and selfish is the next greatest limitation to creating a boundary.

Being infatuated with something or someone, holding them up as superior to you will limit your ability to create a boundary.

Trying to uphold a self-image of "goodness" is the final obstacle to creating a boundary.

If you can dissolve these fears, you will have no problem setting boundaries. You may need to do some work on developing your skill in managing the boundaries strategically – which you can look up in this strategy section – but the energy and the power that is necessary to create a boundary will be available to you if you come from a place of power.

What is really interesting is that for most people there will be at least one or two or three areas in their lives in which the fears mentioned above are operative.

So, for instance, you might be really comfortable creating a boundary when somebody insults you or tries to steal your time, but when it comes to money you may have a belief that you shouldn't look like a "money grubber" or "stingy" or whatever belief system you have around this that prevents you from creating the boundary.

I have mentioned that people tend to have two problems in life, that they are either too nice or too nasty. The need to appear nice and to not offend someone is critical here.

In *The Girl with the Dragon Tattoo* story, it is the inability of the hero to trust his instincts that is the problem. The desire not to offend is immensely and overwhelmingly powerful in our society, and this is what dissolves are boundaries.

I have worked with hundreds of women in abusive relationships who, had they trusted their instincts, would have exited these relationships.

IDENTITY

My mother taught me that having strong opinions meant that you had "character". She was right. What she never discussed, but implied, was that having character was a good thing. And it is, but only up to a point. From then on, it's catastrophic!

Let me explain.

We need a strong identity to both survive in the world and to prevent others from overpowering us. If you want to Awaken spiritually, you have to let go of your identification with your ego, but if you don't have a strong ego to let go of in the first place, you're going to feel like you're going crazy if you start letting go of a fragile ego.

Strong identities create the need to defend themselves, which is the cause of conflict and war. There are endless cries for peace in the world, but this will not happen as long as egos are defending and attacking each other.

A strong identity, a sense of being a "somebody", has to carry with it a fear of losing itself. It is a contracted and desperate attempt to construct, artificially, a sense of who we are. Why is it artificial? Because the identity is a bunch of concepts and labels and ideas attached to our essential nature. An infant has no sense of identity; it is just *being*.

The sense of *being* is not constructed or created in the mind.

It is not an idea.

It is a fact.

Imagine a jar of apricot jam. It has a label on it that says "Apricot jam". How much in common does the label have with the contents of the jar?

Almost nothing. The sticky, sweet, orange contents are a universe away from a couple of squiggles on a piece of paper that is the label. Yet human beings think that they are the label attributed to them: man, woman, husband, wife, lawyer, plumber, father, rugby fanatic, woman's rights activist, writer, bookkeeper, "I believe in this or that," etc.

What we spend most of our lives doing is developing our identity, which is just a series of labels, ideas and feelings, which we now have to rate and score and to which we have to attach our Self-Esteem. And this is what I have been calling Acquired Self-Esteem.

> *Original Self-Esteem is the jam. Acquired Self-Esteem is the label. Most people spend their entire lives totally alienated from the "jam", the "being-ness", that they are.*

If you are no longer identified with your label – it is simply something that is of functional value some of the time – then you are free to be Pure Consciousness, the being-ness, that is the "jam": Original Self-Esteem.

THE HORRORS OF SOCIALISATION

When our parents socialise us and they tell us to be good and kind and nice and sweet and respectful. What's missing in the instruction is the opposing element: to know when to be tough.

If you have kids, what you want to do is help them to learn to be good and kind and respectful, but you also need to teach them – and this is an ongoing dialogue – how to learn to use their instincts to protect themselves and to not let the fear of offending others control them.

We can teach our kids to be well socialised from two potential positions. The one can be to create a fear of offending others – which is the predominant position in our culture – or we can teach kindness to others because we simply *really want to be kind*.

There need not be fear involved in being kind.

So in the second form we do it, not from a place of fear, but from a place of our inherent goodness.

A LIST

Here is a list of just some of the ways in which people will take advantage of someone who is disempowered:

• Bully you with their opinions and needs.

  If you don't have a sense of power around your intellect, ideas, needs and position in arguments you will let other people overpower you. If you fear offending them and need to be liked too much you will let them overpower you in this regard.

- Take your money.

  I was taught that money was the root of all evil, that money was dirty. I was taught the phrase *filthy lucre,* that rich people were largely speaking "Scrooges" and that the nice guys come last. I was also taught to be wealthy! There was a massive contradiction here. I was told to be nice, but that winning was absolutely the number-one thing.

  Pro-depressants at work here, methinks.

- Steal your time – drain your energy.

  Most people, who are bored in conversation, or have another appointment to get to, think it's rude to say "I need to go now", or "I'm not sure what you are trying to tell me", or "No, I don't want to meet to talk to you about your divorce again".

  This is politeness in the wrong place. It is showing respect when it is inappropriate. Our parents teach us respect but they don't teach us that we need to be respectful up to a point and then boundaried thereafter, and that depends on who we are dealing with and how much of our time and energy that person is stealing.

- Underpay you.

  Again, we have so many issues around money that we find it difficult to say that we deserve to be paid more. We subordinate ourselves to people and so we can't ask for more money. We are also very scared of looking arrogant and demanding. So we would rather be exploited than look arrogant. This fear runs us very strongly in relation to money.

  As you know, I'm Jewish and one of the prejudices about Jews is that they are stingy and will always push for a discount. This prejudice made me anxious about appearing stingy and yet, at the same time, my mother taught me to always demand a discount. Another source of my confusion and depression.

The way out of this contradiction for me was to simply use my judgement in the moment as to whether I would ask for a discount and speak up when I felt that somebody was taking advantage of me and to have no interest in the "Jewish" issue.

- Exploit you.

A great deal has been written about learning how to say no. The primary reasons for not saying no is that we don't want to look selfish, create conflict and we don't want to offend. If you can dissolve these needs, then you are home free.

People will offend us and respect us our entire lives. We will respect others and offend them our entire lives. We have a resistance to this reality. We are addicted to harmony. When there is offence there is potential conflict. If you have no resistance to conflict ... this is freedom.

- Use you as a punch bag to make them feel good.

The only reason that bullies are everywhere in the world is that we give them permission to treat us this way.

We allow it.

We are so busy being respectful.

We are so desperate not to offend, even when we are being offended.

We are preserving an image of "goodness".

We are so addicted to being respectful that we are giving them permission to be abusive.

I have had two major conflicts in my 18 years as a corporate consultant. Both had the same cause: I was being disrespected. In both instances I allowed the disrespect to continue for too long; my boundary was too slow in emerging. When my boundary did emerge it led to me exiting the one relationship, and in the other relationship, with the person owning their issues, we were able to continue working together.

I have worked with hundreds of women in my private practice over the years who have been in abusive relationships with men.

I always ask them how early on in the relationship they knew that this man was a self-righteous bully. Most of them, if they're honest, tell me that they knew it in the first week, *but they never challenged it.* Sometimes it's a little longer. Many deny knowing for months, I think they are ... in denial.

They feared being offensive, disrespectful and being more powerful than this very overpowering man.

Notice, I didn't say that the woman *caused the abuse,* although on many occasions the woman provokes the abuse. Provoking is not causing.

One particular woman was having an argument with her boyfriend and she took his very expensive sound system, picked it up and threw it on the floor. He started to beat her. I'm not condoning his abuse, but what I am saying is that this woman could have walked out, rather than escalating the conflict by destroying his sound system.

Here's my bottom line. The biggest problem women have with abusive men is that they don't challenge the abuse *the first time it occurs* and then walk out if it continues.

If nobody ever took any abuse whatsoever, the abusers could not continue.

But the problem is that we are all prostitutes – just in different forms. We are all selling our souls for money, or intimacy, or security, or safety or "image". Prostitution is a pejorative term. We are conditioned to believe that it is bad.

I disagree. Prostitution is a trait, a way of being in the world that we all engage in to avoid problems or gain some kind of advantage or just to survive. To love ourselves for no reason is to love ourselves in our moments or times of prostitution.

I have worked with many of the major financial institutions in South Africa. One of the senior managers once said to me: "Why does our business treat our employees so badly?" I replied: "Because the employees let them!"

Someone can only abuse our boundaries if we let them. There is no judgement here, because we all live in fear and we all live disempowered some of the time and so this leads us to need the pay cheque or the security or the sense of not being abandoned, and these needs collapse our boundaries.

• Prove you wrong.

We live in a head-based culture – as I've discussed. So logic is King and when logic is King we all want to occupy the throne.

Many people are pedantic and logic-based and we need to build our power in this arena by proving to others that we are right and they are wrong. Personally, this has been one of my favoured means of self-protection. My father used to call me a "smart Alec."

He was right!

Believing we are right gives us a sense of Acquired Self-Esteem and we become addicted to it.

I was using my 'smart-Alecness' to gain some power over a very authoritarian man.

We are endlessly faced with people who want to prove us wrong. If you don't have a good boundary, you will let them win. It doesn't mean you have to win back. You just have to show them that you don't agree with them and if you can do this with an energetic signature that is calm and powerful, that's great.

- Manipulate you into buying things you don't want.

This is a double-edged monster. We want new things because we think they will give us more happiness. So the more new things that we have, the more happiness we think we will acquire. Everywhere, somone is wanting to sell us something and so our fear of not having enough happiness leads us to buy. We also don't want to reject them – the fear of offending is again paramount

To create this boundary, what we need to do is see through the illusion that says that we will be happier when we have this thing and then dissolve our fear of offending.

- Want to make you feel bad, inferior, stupid.

People do this all the time. Why? Because they feel inferior, and the only way to protect themselves from their sense of inferiority is to make themselves feel superior. The only way that they can get away with it is if you believe them.

If you don't feel good enough without approval and without success, then you are essentially saying: "I feel inferior until I succeed or until I'm approved of and so I will let you abuse me because it agrees with my perception of myself." You are asking the world to abuse you and to make you feel bad.

Our capacity to feel guilt simply exacerbates this problem. Guilt is only necessary if you think that it's the only way you are going to grow and behave "better".

If you believe that growth and goodness can come from a place other than feeling bad about yourself, then a potentially different scenario arises.

- Get you to do things you don't want to do.

If your friend wants to borrow your lawnmower and you have had bad experiences with this in the past, then lending him your lawnmower is going to depress and anger you. You also have a fear that it will threaten your friendship with him, and yes, it might.

The Lawnmower Syndrome says that you lend your friend your lawnmower. He borrows it on the Friday, and you say you want it back on the Sunday. He calls you on the Sunday to say his car is broken down and he can't return it, so now you have to fetch it from him.

You've done him a favour, but you now you are burdened and irritated. That is simply the way it is. Doing somebody a favour does not mean that you are going to be rewarded in the way you want to and it doesn't mean you won't be inconvenienced.

If you now stop lending people your lawnmower, you look selfish.

The Lawnmower Syndrome says: "If you do someone a favour, expect to be inconvenienced". This is somewhat like the exaggerated expression: "No good deed goes unpunished". This is only sometimes true.

It is useful to know this because we have this fantasy that being good or kind or helpful to others is *entirely* positive, that we will be rewarded for it.

IN CONFIDENCE

I love those moments when somebody says to me, leaning forward surreptitiously across the coffee table: "Can I tell you something in confidence?"

In the past I used to say yes, and I was disempowered.

Now I say: "I don't think that's a good idea until I know what it is you want to tell me. I would be betraying myself if I offered you my confidence when I don't know the content of what I'm agreeing to. It's like signing a contract without reading it."

People look shocked when I say this, but doesn't it make sense? You want me to offer you my confidence and I don't even know what I'm offering it for! This is not a boundary.

THE MILLGRAM EXPERIMENT

There was a most extraordinary and controversial psychological experiment conducted by Stanley Millgram at Yale University in 1961. It was designed to assess people's compliance or obedience to authority under extreme duress.

It would never have been conducted today because it would be considered unethical in the extreme. Many of the participants were deeply traumatised by the experience.

Millgram wanted to try and understand why the German people could permit the extermination of the Jews during the Second World War. Many Germans, in response to this question said:

"I was simply following orders."

Essentially it was a test of how powerful people's psychological boundaries are under pressure, a great measure of Self-Esteem or personal power.

Subjects were seated in a chair and asked to administer shocks to someone behind a one-way mirror. The person being shocked had increasing degrees of shock administered to them as they gave incorrect answers to questions regarding the pairing of words.

Unbeknown to the subject, the person being shocked was an accomplice of the experimenters and was only pretending to be shocked.

A man in a white coat would urge the subject to increase the voltage of the shocks given up to 450 volts, despite cries of desperation from the accomplice.

What is so disturbing is that 65% of the subjects administered shocks up to the 450 volt maximum.

In other words, nearly two-thirds of human beings appear to have no boundary around inflicting serious harm on another person, when urged to do so by a person in a position of authority.

The majority of people are without power, without a psychological boundary when placed in front of a person who is perceived as having greater authority than them.

This is really not very surprising to me. As children we are forced to do multitudes of things we don't want to do but we feel that we have to do, by parents, teachers and adults in general. We are trained not to have boundaries.

My schooling experience was, for me, like a prison. I really hated most aspects of it. All I learned there was reading, writing and arithmetic. I think I could have learnt this in about three or four years, not the 12 that was inflicted upon me, and the most important point is that, given the choice, I would not have wanted to be there!

Nobody asks you if you want to go to school. To do something against one's will is to have a collapsed psychological boundary. Of course, when this happens we are children and it's understandable that we have to succumb to this pressure.

There are multitudes of other ways in which children are denied their needs. Ways in which their boundaries are breached. They are told to eat all of the food on their plate, to eat their vegetables, to stop watching television and go to bed, to go to church and to the synagogue and the mosque, to do as they are told.

The life of the child is in many ways about having to adapt to a set of rules and norms created by adults. We have no choice in the matter.

In essence we are trained to not have psychological boundaries – it is a fact of life.

And so we learn to submit to authority, to people more powerful than us. We learn subordination, and this erodes our Esteem. It is unavoidable.

Of course, children can rebel. Those who rebel have a tremendous advantage over those who don't, as long as the rebellion isn't excessive. There is no question that excessive compliance is correlated with low Self-Esteem. The problem with excessive rebellion is that the identity one develops is established in *contradiction* to others.

It is not a unique expression of individuality; it is individuality in *opposition to* authority and so it doesn't have its own identity.

To put it another way, rebellion simply fights anyone in authority irrespective of the validity of the position of the person in authority.

So the bottom line here is:

What happens to your power, under pressure from someone else?

Biologically we automatically create boundaries. As infants when we are in pain or when we are hungry or thirsty we cry, we let the world know that we have a problem. We don't have to think about it, we don't have a cerebral cortex yet which can do the thinking.

And then our parents start to tell us when we express our needs as we grow up that we are "naughty, demanding, difficult, selfish, pushy, mean" and so on.

And so the socialisation process which is, of course, necessary, as I've discussed, in order to create some sense of order in society, starts to block the expression of our needs, our power.

We become over-socialised good boys and girls.

One of the biggest problems I've seen in organisations is that most people go into the Victim position of Retreat when they're under pressure or threat. In other words, they're so frightened of expressing their authenticity and power that they hide and go into silence and pretend that everything is fine.

In relationships people are infatuated at the beginning and only express their exaggerated appreciation of their partner. And then when they get disappointed they flip to the other side and start to fight in an inappropriately aggressive way.

I often say that there are two problems in the world: people are too nice and too nasty to each other. Which are the Attack and Retreat victim positions.

Attack is an exaggerated expression of a boundary and Retreat is the inability to express a boundary.

The people who live a great deal in the Attack position seldom come and see me for help.

Why?

Because for them their problems are "caused by other people"; it's never them.

In my coaching practice, I have often been referred business executives to work with by the CEO of a company, who is predominantly attacking others.

People like this destroy teams.

I'm not particularly fond of working with these people, because their motivation to change is very low.

They're not interested in growing.

They're interested in pointing out what's wrong with everybody else.

It is the people in the Retreat position who struggle with boundaries, who are sensitive to conflict and aggression, who really want to do the work, and I love working with them. They are much more open to feedback and really want to learn to connect with their power.

BUILDING POWER FOR BOUNDARIES

I remember so clearly living in terror of dating girls when I was 18 or 19 years old.

What would I talk about?

Would they like me?

If they did like me, then how would I make a decision to hold their hands or kiss them and what if they rejected me...horror of horrors?

I loved the line from *Annie Hall,* where Woody Allen is on a date with Diane Keaton and they're walking to the restaurant for dinner and he says:

"Gimme a kiss", and she says: "Really?" and he replies: "Yes, 'cause we're just gonna go home later and there's gonna be all that tension you know, we've never kissed before and I'll never know when to make the right move, so we'll kiss now, we'll get it over with and go eat, OK? We'll digest our food better." And she agrees and they kiss.

I loved that because I was so filled with just that kind of anxiety, endlessly!

These days I have different anxieties. It's called *The Law of Conservation of Anxiety.* It's conserved across your entire lifetime – it doesn't go away!

The bottom line here is that as an 18-year-old, I was utterly disempowered around women. Why? Because I was so infatuated with the idea of getting close to one of them, of being with one of them, of kissing one of them, of making love to one of them. The infatuation completely immobilised me.

This infatuation is perfectly illustrated in the response of a six-year-old girl to the question, "What is love?"

She replied: "Love is when two people go out on their first date and tell each other a bunch of lies!"

They tell the lies because they're infatuated!

People get very upset when we lie to them. Well, when we create fantasies *we are lying to ourselves!*

But whoever owns that?

And so it's really useful to notice when you are infatuated in your relationships, because your infatuation will immobilise you and destroy your boundary.

Let's say you can think of nothing better than meeting a famous movie star – say Angelina Jolie or Meryl Streep or George Clooney or Ashton Kutcher – and you go to Hollywood and you bump into them. Your infatuation, which is elevating them above yourself and making you believe you are inferior, is going to leave you speechless and you will have no boundary.

If they asked you to run naked across Hollywood Boulevard, you'd probably do it even though you didn't want to. That's what a lack of power and a collapsed boundary does.

The primary way in which we disempower ourselves in relationships is to perceive someone else as more important than us, cleverer than us, more beautiful or attractive than us, more successful than us ... and then you will disempower yourself and you will invite them in to overpower you.

Your boundaries will dissolve.

So the answer is very simple. Think of the people who fit any of the above categories of superiority and start to bring in your power in relation to them and notice how you start to become more genuine and authentic with them.

Dissolve all of your inferiorities and anxieties in power and your marshmallow nature will dissolve.

TOO NICE TOO NASTY

I want to talk a little bit more about this "too nice, too nasty" thing.

What I've noticed about people and myself, particularly in the past, is that when we don't create boundaries and we are too nice and we let people overpower us, we build this resentment inside, and once this resentment has grown enough, we can then explode with indignation and anger and overexpress the boundary.

This is what most people do in relationships.

If one had appropriate boundaries, one would be sharing these difficulties with one's partner and then finally, when the time comes to leave, one would say in a modulated and calm way:

"I'm afraid I just can't live with our problematic relationship anymore and I really need to leave."

Very few people do this, because they spend so much time in the "too nice" position and then flip to the "too nasty" position. This is not an appropriate expression of a boundary.

In my Victim Triangle, it is the two upper elements, Attack and Retreat, that I'm talking about here.

So most conversations between friends around problematic people are an avoidance of simply expressing the boundary *appropriately*.

Great Original Self-Esteem doesn't need to be emotional in order to express its power. *This is a huge mistake in our culture*. We can usually only make big decisions when we are very emotional about them.

Why?

Because we are disempowered. We need a strong emotion to propel us into action. If you have great power, self-love and wisdom, *you can do it without a strong emotion*.

Thinking that you have to be emotional in order to make a big decision is a mistake. If you get into your power, you can just do what you need to do without having to complain about it and moan about it to another person.

Wise and skilful action simply emerges spontaneously from you.

> *Great boundaries are simply a spontaneous expression of your authenticity. Poor boundaries are a lack of this spontaneity.*

TWO ELEMENTS

There are two specific elements to building boundaries. The first involves the "internal" *emotional work*, everything I have mentioned above, and involves all of the exercises and techniques to building love of self and creating internal power.

The second is learning the strategies around *how* to build boundaries, which I call *Strategic Questions*. You can go to the technique section in order to do this.

Go to chapter 18 for the strategy.

CHAPTER 8

RECLAIMING LOVE & POWER: A MEDITATIVE JOURNEY

RECLAIMING MY SPIRIT

When I was this joyous child, I knew nothing.
I was empty, expectant
A blank slate for you to write upon.
And write you did,
Horrors did you teach
And I believed it all and donated away all of my power.

Now is my time
Like a trumpet to the heavens
To call it back
To see it fill me to brimming over
With delight
This vital spirit energy
Glowing, burning with love and delight!

Mark Peter Kahn.

It is really an amazing thing to discover that every time your Self-Esteem dips or crashes, you are giving away your self-worth, power and Spirit with it. Very few people notice this.

Noticing this is very helpful, because from the noticing can come the transformation. From the noticing can come a decision to start refusing to give your power away and from this comes the potential to *reclaim it!*

It has fascinated me, this question. Why do we give away our power, to situations and to other people? I think there are multiple reasons:

As children we come shining into the world with Original Self-Esteem. We are innocent, spacious, open and delighted with being.

If you were trained in the concept of original sin, you may have great difficulty with this idea. So check who said this to you. Are you sure they were right?

If you think the Bible said it, check: why did Christ wash the feet of the prostitute – clearly a "sinner"?

Can you metaphorically wash your own feet in the face of your imperfections?

Perhaps your idea of sin is incorrect! If so, dissolve this belief in Truth.

But back to being a child. We are criticised, admonished, controlled and abused. Our parents cannot see us as whole and beautiful human beings and they have their own fears and struggles and pain and so the simple statements "be careful", "don't do that", "don't be naughty", "be nice to your sister", "you're lazy, you're fat, you're stupid..." all create the doubt, the uncertainty, the pain, the hurt.

In the moment that we are hurt we contract and in the contraction our power and love and worth leaks out of us. It is given away because we believe that the pain is who we are. We identify with the pain and the hurt and the contraction as our identity. We are so vulnerable and so small that we believe the external world, the people who judge us, who say that we are not okay, and so our true nature, our goodness, is surrendered in favour of the doubt and the judgment of self.

We also give away our self-worth because we do not believe in ourselves. We have not acquired wisdom and knowledge, and so we subordinate ourselves to the power of the adult who is so much bigger than us, stronger than us and on whom we rely for all of our sustenance and survival.

So the beginning of this healing process is to notice that we have made ourselves small and vulnerable and that we live in doubt of ourselves. Can you begin to notice how you have done this and are doing this every day of your life?

Can you notice the energetic signature of doubt, and that in the doubt you surrender and give away your Power to another?

And then can you notice the energetic signature of not believing in the self? How you have surrendered your self to situations and people thousands and thousands of times in your life?

And now you can begin to get the sense of the possibility of being able to reclaim the belief in yourself and to surrender the doubt to the world, as you reclaim your power.

I hope that you are beginning to truly *know* and *feel* and *sense* the immensity of this discovery.

You really want to "get" how you can reclaim the belief and the surrendering of the knowing of what you truly are.

In Part 2 there is a beautiful meditation to work with this process – Chapter 21.

CHAPTER 9

IF ONLY THIS ONE THING WOULD CHANGE ... I WOULD BE HAPPY

"My life will really, really start when this next problem is sorted!"

"The game never ends when your whole world depends,

on the turn of a friendly card."

The Alan Parson's Project.

"The fantasy that we can solve the next problem and the next one and the

next one and be then be happy ... is an interminable delusion of agony."

"If you feel good or bad because of what's going to happen next,

you're toast."

"Nothing can make you happy

Until

NOTHING can make you happy."

Jeff Foster

LONGING FOR THE NEXT PAINLESS MOMENT

My life will begin when the next thing is done, fixed, finished,
Banished into non-existence.
Oh the relief, the promised land it is
A land of fake lies and fools' dreams
I've woven to balm my fatal pain.

But like waves to a rocky shore
Coming, they keep coming
The pain, the inconvenience, coming
keeping coming, never ending,
Infinite always returning.

I feel like Sisyphus straining against the tide
Which always turns
Everywhere I turn, it turns against me such
Sinewed stretching, fighting angst.

To fight and fight and to stay hopeful always hopeful
Hope is good they say and yet
I see hope turned to despair again, again,
again each wave of hope turned,
Soured, crashed and burning
Cinders...
To rise again, hopeless and fulfilled,
Returned to the Source of life of Being-ness.

Mark Peter Kahn.

The ruminative mind is locked into telling stories. That's all it does.

If you are in the past, or in the future, ruminating about them, you are outside of the only thing that exists, the present.

The mind has nothing to do in the present; it is out of a job when you are in the present.

It's idle and it cannot tolerate that, so the ruminative mind's job is to kill us by taking us on trips into the past or the future.

When we resist the present, we often wish that this one thing would change and then when it changes, we will be happy. The weekend, new job, the relationship, the holiday, when the illness is over. The list is endless.

"My life will start when this thing is fixed."

This is what we believe so much of the time. But the "thing" gets fixed and then the next problem arises. That is why the Alan Parsons line, *"The game never ends when your whole world depends on the turn of a friendly card"*, is so beautiful. And that is why our games never end. Always waiting for the next pain to leave and the next great thing to happen.

So the question arises: can I just dissolve the future in love and stay here now, just this now, right here, only this? Wow!!!!!

Why does the present make me sad? Because as soon as I think the future has something special, then the present is not good! I resent and resist whatever is happening now. Can you honour this "Now", whatever is happening in it?

One of the great dissolving processes is therefore to dis-assemble the desire to go backwards or forwards in time.

We think about this evening and we remember that a great sports game is on TV or we have to work and so we get alternatively happy or sad and that is the end of us. Although the future doesn't exist, this virtual reality in our heads can make us feel good or bad. It's a wonderful and terrible delusion.

GRIEF AND LOSS

We love birth and beginnings and we hate endings. But life is essentially birth and death, not just of the body and things, but all of the good times end and so do the bad times. Everything, in each moment is being birthed and is dying. Can you honour this reality?

Grief is a resistance to this reality.

There is a most beautiful story of a Zen monk. An old man lives on a hill above a town.

A young student who is wealthy comes to see him and enjoys the connection and the teachings that he gets from the monk. One day he gives the monk a beautiful and very expensive crystal goblet, which the monk puts on his window sill and uses often.

One day one of his students says: "Are you not anxious that one day this goblet will get broken?"

And the monk replies: "Yes indeed. One day the wind will blow or somebody's arm or clothing will brush against the goblet and it will fall to the floor and break and I will shed a tear and then I will say 'Of course, what else'. And so now I say, the goblet is already broken."

This is the most exquisite story about how to deal with loss. What is so interesting is that I saw this story posted on Facebook on Francis Bennett's page and one of the comments about the story was: "Yes, that's non-attachment."

And someone responded most wisely saying: "No. It's not about non-attachment. It's about being completely connected *and being able to let go* and so the monk still sheds a tear but underneath that he is saying that the goblet is already broken."

And that's the point. It's not an unemotional disconnected state. It is saying that the transience of life makes it special and wonderful, and if you buy into birth and death, then the tear is shed, there is a momentary sense of loss. But then one falls back into the knowing that the goblet is already broken and so "Of course, what else" is known, which is saying there is no resistance to death and change.

If you can stop clinging to the goodness and resent and resist the badness and loss, then you are free of the Victim consciousness that arises out of resistance to loss, and death and grief will be but momentary.

INSPIRED VS DESPERATE WANTING

It is a fantasy that the next thing that we are hoping will happen, will make us permanently happy, and the mind also endlessly looks for what's missing. Oscar Wilde said:

"There are two problems in life, not getting what you want and getting what you want."

If he is right, and I believe he is, then perhaps "wanting" is the problem. I puzzled about this issue for years and years. So much is written about "wanting" being a problem and yet it is so much a part of our nature.

When I started to create this Self-Esteem work, I had a great realisation. There are two kinds of wanting: desperate wanting and inspired wanting.

Desperate wanting comes from Acquired Self-Esteem. It is filled with the anxiety of wanting something too badly. Inspired wanting is Original Self-Esteem. It comes from a deeper place inside of us. It has a breadth and depth and a purity to it.

Desperate wanting comes from pain and a sense of lack.

It is a *contraction* into the future.

Inspired wanting is an *expansion* into the future.

Huge difference!

Desperate wanting is like that beautiful line of psychology from the movie *Cool Runnings*.

It's about the Jamaican bobsled team that makes it to the 1988 Winter Olympics in Calgary in Canada. It's of course amusing and deeply ironic because Jamaica has no snow and absolutely zero history of bobsledding!

The Jamaicans are busy qualifying when it's discovered that their coach Irv Blitzer, who had two gold medals from winter Olympics 16 years previously, was disqualified in his third Olympics for cheating.

There is a huge controversy about this and the Jamaicans are potentially going to be ejected from the games. While the controversy is in full swing one of the Jamaican team members approaches the coach and says in a truly exasperated and upset way:

"But coach, you already had two gold medals. Why did you have to cheat to get a third one?"

And here is the beautiful line:

> *"A gold medal is a wonderful thing,*
> *but if you're not enough without it,*
> *you'll never be enough with it."*

The cheating behind the wanting of the third gold medal was clearly, for Irv Blitzer, *desperate*. He needed it to make himself feel better. There was no belief in himself, no sense that he was okay without the gold medal *and that two gold medals were not enough to boost his Self-Esteem permanently.* There was probably little inspiration in his performance, it was rather a desperateness that fuelled his desire.

So much of our lives looks like what Irv Blitzer was doing when he cheated. Of course, the seeds of his cheating were there before he cheated. If your Self-Esteem depends on the outcome of the next thing that is going to happen in your life, you are lost.

Our culture encourages desperateness. We are told that we are okay if we are number one, if we are brilliant, if we are beautiful, if we are thin, if we are able to make a certain amount of money. In essence, we are not good enough as we are. We have to become something else and so we have to *have* something else in order to be okay.

Many years ago I was running a group psychotherapy workshop – once-a-week sessions for about three months. One of the participants, a woman, said at the end of the process: "I have realised something very important. I am enough as I am."

So we are looking to the next thing to make us happy. And, of course, you've noticed that the happiness lasts for minutes, perhaps hours, perhaps days.

Some years ago I went out for lunch with a friend who is just getting divorced and it was a very traumatic time for him and we talked about it over the lunch. When we came out of the restaurant we walked into the car park and he said:

"Do you want to see my new car," and of course I said, "Yes."

And there was this beautiful new Porsche and he smiled very endearingly and said to me: "I bought it to make myself feel better." And I said: "And how long did the good feeling last." And he said, smiling:

"One week!"

We have an almost knee-jerk response, thinking "Oh, I want the latest upgrade on my cellphone, or that new app or that new piece of software that's just a click away, or that perfect partner or two kids or the dream home … and then I will be happy, then I will feel better". But the real happiness, the lasting, deep, resonant happiness never comes, not for long.

Nothing wrong with having these things, but they will ultimately not bring the happiness, the peace, the sense of being "enough" that we expect.

Go to chapter 22 for the strategy.

CHAPTER 10

Projecting Self-Esteem

Such longing for the beauty and love and power that I see,
Always on the outside
Always excruciatingly out of reach
Always in something or someone else.

Will it ever be mine to hold and cherish
And wear as a badge of honour
To puff up my ego, miserable mannequin
Sad, poor soul, not a Soul at all.
Just a deluded-ness, rampant, running through the grass
Searching for the truth on the outside.

To return home is key.
To discover, reveal, unveil the beauty within,
The relief.
The searching over.
I am all things lauded out there.

The eye looks inward, sighs,
"I am complete."

Mark Peter Kahn.

"We project our darkness and our light out into the world.
Dissolve the darkness and re-own the light."

Freud discovered that projection is a mechanism designed to deal with the pain of certain experiences and traits. We dislike our selfishness, our cruelty, our laziness, our manipulativeness, our dishonesty ... the list is endless.

All of these so-called negative traits we project onto others because it is too painful to honour within. It is a distortion of reality, because we don't want to see ourselves as we are. What's interesting is that projection is one of the most powerful defence mechanisms that people engage in and yet very few people are able to own their projections.

If you say to somebody, when they're criticising another person for being selfish: "Are you not just perhaps projecting your own selfishness onto the other person?"

You are likely to get a very defensive response.

I'm a psychologist and for decades I really struggled to see my own projections.

One of the reasons for this is that we generally project onto a person who *does* have the characteristics we are projecting and so it's very easy to be seduced by the obviousness of the "problem" in *them* and to not see it in *ourselves* as well.

In other words, if you don't like to be seen as manipulative, you are going to project that trait of manipulativeness onto someone who is *indeed* manipulative.

In creating this work, to my surprise, I discovered that we also project our Self-Esteem onto others and the world.

As soon as we subordinate ourselves to somebody, we think we're inferior to them. We have disowned our positive value and projected it onto the person we admire or envy.

This was most beautifully illustrated in a piece of corporate work I was doing a while back.

I was working with a team with two young women, who were friends, vying for the same promotion. I was in the room when their superior entered and told one of them that she had attained the position. Her friend turned to her and said: "God you are amazing ... I hate you."

There was a very special honesty about the statement, which contained the subordination and inferiority simultaneously, in saying "You are amazing" and "I hate you". All of us are doing this all of the time and very often simultaneously, but usually outside of our awareness.

Social media encourages and escalates this tendency. Everyone else is having a wonderful time but you aren't. Their lives are filled with abundance and yours is the opposite. FOMO – fear of missing out – is created by Facebook.

I like to call it FBE, Facebook Envy, which means I don't have the fantastic life that you *appear* to be having right now ... and so I am deflated and inferior and I'm filled with envy for what appears to be the better life you are having.

A while back, for a period of two weeks, I looked at pictures on Facebook of a friend of mine who was traveling on a yacht in the Mediterranean. It was one azure blue sky after another, pictures of beautiful meals with glistening glasses of wine, one after another ... at exquisite dockside cafés with beautiful white Greek houses nestling on hillsides above the sea, one after another!

So I privately Facebook messaged my friend and said: "It looks like you're having the most amazing time. Are there any downsides?" (I knew that there had to be downsides because nothing on the planet is all "upsides".) To which she replied:

"Yes it is absolutely wonderful, but my in-laws are hard work!"

What's interesting is that when we're going through our friends' posts on Facebook, we are going to be projecting our

Self-Esteem onto them as well as projecting our negative traits onto them.

So when we read a post that has a joke that we don't like, we are going to judge it as superficial or not funny. Which is probably a projection of our own superficiality that we judge in ourselves. And then in the next moment we are going to be envying someone else who's doing the Greek island cruise or Paris in the spring.

Both forms of projection are happening within moments of each other.

I will share with you a most beautiful and simple process to connect with innocence in the strategy section – Chapter 23.

CHAPTER 11

From Pain to Love & Power 2.0

"To reclaim your self worth is to become who you truly are."

I AM WORTHY

It is so simple
No fancy alchemy
No mystical, magical, conjuror's device.

The pain inserted
Now removed.
Bloodless surgery
Gone like the night
"I am worthy."
As the sun rises in the East.

Mark Peter Kahn.

Let's assume that you are struggling in your work as a manager. You are not good at managing difficult subordinates. You get frustrated and angry too quickly and you don't pay enough attention to the relationship, but focus on the operational issues, i.e. getting the job done. It isn't easy for you to build trust with problematic subordinates.

The reason that this is a problem is because of your early relationship with an abusive teacher. Under pressure you tend to shut down, get angry and defensive and lose sight of the other person's needs. You become consumed with your own issues and forget to work on the *relationship*.

So the ongoing problem with subordinates, which is a pain in the present, is really a reflection of the pain with the schoolteacher. The two are inseparable.

So use pain in the present to trace back to issues from the past that you have probably forgotten about. In the same way as you release more issues from the past, your energy becomes softer and easier and looser as you reconnect with your power now.

Another really important thing to do is when you make your list of issues in the present, look for how these issues are a reflection of who you are, as opposed to what's wrong with the world. For example, one of your issues in the present might be that your partner doesn't listen to you or is disconnected from you. Now you may be right – they are not listening well and they may be disconnected from you – but if you focus on wanting to change them, you're going to be stuck in the Victim position for ever.

The work is to establish what them not listening to you evokes in you and where that pain comes from and how it makes you feel when you're not listened to, and to trace that back into the past.

If you weren't listened to as a child and you went into pain, you then dropped your power. What you need to do is reclaim your power as a child, when you were not listened to.

This is not an easy thing to do. Our tendency is to look externally and to blame and judge the person on the outside for evoking our pain, and then what we start to do is wonder whether this relationship is good for us or not and this leads into deep ruminations about our ability to succeed in a relationship or not and really it is a tangled web of ruminations and stories and pain, which lead us ... nowhere.

So unfortunately this takes a great deal of discipline, because the tendency to blame the other person is very powerful. Why? Because it is much easier to do than it is to go inside and do the work on finding one's power when one was not listened to as a child.

One of the questions that people in intimate relationships ask themselves in the incessant storytelling around this kind of problem is: "Is this person the right one for me?"

And my answer to you here is: "Do the work on yourself first. Heal the pain around not being listened to and then decide whether this person is the right person for you or not."

What I find with most of my clients is if they heal the pain of not being listened to, at least partially, then they can love their partner as they are and they usually don't need to move on. This isn't always the case but certainly it is a possible outcome.

Obviously there are many other issues and this is much more complicated than not being listened to. Our fantasies create an expectation that our partner will fulfil needs for us in a multitude of areas. That they will be excited about the same things as us, that they will be interested in the same things as us, that they will have the same values as us about how to treat people and that they will honour our families of origin in the way that we want them to, that when we are sick or stressed they will either let us be or be very nurturing – whichever it is that we want most.

Another one of the great things I learned from Dr Demartini is that people can only love us in terms of their values, which means that they can only show caring in the ways they're able to, based on the structure of their personality.

If you try to get them to love you in ways that are not aligned with their personalities, the result is usually endless conflict and you will drive yourself crazy.

MANAGING CRISES

What often happens with this Self-Esteem work, is that you're doing very well and then you hit a crisis. You get sick. There are many problems, your partner isn't well, your kids are doing badly at school or develop some emotional issue, whatever it is and it is very feasible that you might wobble and struggle to implement the techniques that have been working for you.

One of the reasons for this is that we are often habituated to managing stress by going into shock, or panic, or simply by going into the victim position because we've done it thousands and thousands of times before.

So you simply go into the stress response as you have done in the past.

What I recommend is the following. Recover as best you can in the time that you can and be kind to yourself. Except that it may take you time and then what you want to do is go back to the trauma or the stress and work with it as you would in dissolving pain from the past. Because now this has become something in the past even if it was only yesterday or a few days ago.

RISK VS AVOIDANCE ANXIETY

"A ship in the harbour is safe - but its nature, its purpose,
is not lived when resting there."

"If that which we avoid is greater
than that which we confront ... we die..."
Adapted paraphrasing of the words of Ben Okri.

I want to talk about risk and avoidance.

It is an extraordinarily important issue in most people's lives.

We spend an immense amount of time in avoidance of the pain that is locked deep in our hearts. Then we have to navigate our way through relationships and situations in order to avoid having this pain being activated.

This is avoidance anxiety.

When we face the pain and dissolve it, we can risk ourselves more actively in the world, growing psychologically and spiritually.

In the workshops I have run over the years, I have regularly asked participants, "Who of you have stayed too long in a job or in a relationship?" 90% of people put up their hands; the other 10% are thinking about whether to own up or not!

In essence, all of us have experienced the pain of stagnation, of not moving when we need to. People say that they don't know what else to do, they are scared of moving on, their anxiety paralyses them. Scared financially and emotionally, they don't know if things will work out etc...

They describe the risks of shifting in all sorts of detail. All of these people are choosing the pain of stagnation. When you buy into the idea that there has to be pain and risk and fear when you move into anything new, you make it easier to move. In a sense, when we stagnate we are valuing security higher than fulfilment. When you value fulfilment higher than security, you can take the risk.

So one thing to do is dissolve your need for security!

NOT SPEAKING THE TRUTH

One of the top three biggest problems that I see in business meetings is that people avoid speaking their truth, for two primary reasons: they fear conflict and they don't have the ability to say what they want to say *skilfully*.

In life in general people have an immense avoidance around having difficult conversations and doing the things that create anxiety in them.

What this means is that life offers us multitudes of opportunities to either avoid doing what is threatening to us, or risk doing what is threatening to us. If you know that you want to move out of your occupation, or if you know that you need to remove a problematic individual from your team, or if you want to expand your business into new areas, or risk pushing for promotion, whatever the risk, there has to be anxiety.

If you are anxious about a conversation you need to have with a friend or with a family member, the avoidance of this conversation is going to drive you nuts.

Everyone has had the experience where they did not speak the truth, where they went into silence or retreat and did not say what they authentically felt. Going into Retreat will destroy your energy. It is deeply debilitating and disempowering.

The more you avoid in your life, the more you are disempowered.

There is a large piece of double-sidedness to this story. If you want something better, if you want something new, there has to be risk involved in getting it.

There is no such thing as a "free lunch".

The more avoidance anxiety you choose in your life, the more debilitating it is for you on a multitude of levels. The more you choose skilful risk anxiety in your life, the more fulfilment and improved Original Self-Esteem you are likely to have.

I say "likely" because if you risk impulsively or unskilfully, that too can create chaos.

Simply notice how much of the time you avoid risking yourself and see if you can move this into *taking* the risks. You cannot have growth without stagnation. No human being can grow all of the time. If you tried to grow all of the time, you would burn out! You are going to have both in your life.

So in reality, we risk, we relax and recover, we risk again, maybe we stagnate a bit, which is *too* much recovery, and then we risk again.

Every time you experience pain you have the choice of contracting against it and trying to shut down – losing your power – or opening to it and releasing it. The more you contract against pain, the more likely you are to go into avoidance and avoidance creates deep stagnation.

The bottom line here is that you are not going to live a life without anxiety. But you have a choice, whether it comes in the form of risk or avoidance.

Living in avoidance anxiety creates low Self-Esteem, depression, guilt and a lack of fulfilment. Living more in risk anxiety creates high Self-Esteem, fulfilment and fewer emotional issues.

There is a danger that you can engage in risk anxiety, but in a very contracted "tight" form.

I saw movie recently in which somebody suggested that another person run straight towards what scares them the most, which has a kind of macho tone to it and that is not healthy. In fact, I think that many "successful" people live like this, throwing themselves off the cliff of "risk" on a daily basis, but being very tense, contracted and tight about it. Much of the time they are probably in Acquired Self-Esteem and are risking from this place.

Go to Chapter 24 for the strategy.

CHAPTER 12

I Only Exist if You Approve of Me.

"Where is the source of love, for you?"

You gave me a name
You laughed when I smiled
You fed me, clothed me
Gave me words to speak
You gave me labels for everything
Things to call "Mine,"

Books and movies and toys to teach
My fingers and hands and eyes to
Manipulate and create, to make things.

You hugged me and held me and kissed me,
Stilled my troubled heart.

But I came to exist because you noticed me
The trap door on my freedom slammed shut
Trapped in needing that look in your eye.

I exist because of you
Handcuffed, condemned, prisoned,
Needy and always, always, always looking outside.
To discover in your eye ... that I Am.

Can I turn inside to find
The source, the fount, the Origin of my being?
Only there do I resonate like a giant Tibetan gong,
Opening into the great still mountain lake
The Origin of all created.

Mark Peter Kahn.

Do you have any idea of how much of the time in your life your sense of existence is derived externally?

One of the reasons that we hate solitary confinement is that we don't have somebody there to affirm the reality of our existence, the validity of our existence.

When you come into the world as an infant there is no sense of a "me" separate from a you; there is just this vibrating sense of aliveness and consciousness existing in form.

And then slowly we get trained into becoming that which is a separate individual, filled with wants and needs and an identity that needs to be upheld and developed and protected.

The problem is that the sense of identity comes from other people, it comes from outside of us. And that's just the way it is.

The sense of existence that is derived from other people has immense blessings. It enables rewarding connections and contact and warmth and affection and support to be exchanged back and forth. The problem is that the downside is overwhelming. We are always looking for and needing and manipulating the world in order to get the sense that we exist and have validity, from other people.

This makes us vulnerable and dependent and puts us into the Victim position.

To transcend this victimhood is to move into a place where we can truly love ourselves and truly love others. If I feel good because you make me feel good, then I'm going to want to manipulate you to behave in ways that make me feel good again and again and again.

This is useful for survival, but if you want to go beyond survival and you want to transcend into higher levels of consciousness, then you want to go beyond this.

In our culture we love to talk about developing authenticity and a strong sense of identity, but you can't do this if you are addicted to approval from others. This addiction makes you behave in ways that get the approval, that might feel temporarily good but are not aligned with your authenticity.

Yuval Harari has written the most beautiful book called *Sapiens*. He describes one such a contradiction in our culture, which says that we uphold both equality *and* freedom. We can only ensure equality if we take away the freedoms of those who are doing better than others. There are many other contradictions in people's expectations of us, for example:

- Show respect for others, but be authentic.
- Be kind to others, but stand up for your rights.
- Tell the truth, but don't be rude.
- Be good, but be powerful.
- Be creative, but don't break the rules.

The point is that if you listen to what other people say and if your sense of identity is derived from them, you are going to be a basket case.

In addition, the world and people will endlessly approve and disapprove of you, no matter how hard you try to manipulate them – i.e. you will always be rewarded and rejected.

So to define your existence via other people's perceptions is to condemn yourself to self-doubt and Acquired Self-Esteem.

It is not just your fingerprints that are unique, it is all of you that is unique. Any way in which your identity is acquired from others dilutes this uniqueness. And that is why Self-Esteem fluctuates so much. It will go up and down depending on who is approving or disapproving of you at that point in time and it will go up and down depending on whether you are approving of yourself or not.

If your approval of yourself is not defined externally, then this is Original Self-Esteem, and you're home free.

The best way to do this piece of work is meditatively. Go to Chapter 25 for this meditation process.

CHAPTER 13

A Power Poem

AUDIO RECORDING

You can access an audio recording of this poem. If you're reading this as an eBook, you can click on the link below to access the recording. If you are reading this on a hardcopy, type the link into your web browser to access the audio.

http://bit.ly/poemsmeditations

When we are small and shining like the sun
Curious and filled with delight
All things have us wide eyed
And we are amazed at the world of
movement, of colours and things
And power is in our gut.

It was our true nature, this power.
We were filled to overflowing with courage.

Learning to walk,
Falling down, getting up, falling down, getting up.
The word failure nowhere to be found in our lexicon,
We didn't even have a lexicon!

Reaching out into this world of amazement and delight.
There was energy beyond the thinking of it,
Such vitality, diaphanous whirls of light.

Spirit was our name
Soaring eagle like, rising in a spiral vortex,
In the solar plexus.

And then the darkness descended.
The cold and dank and misty corridors of hell
Came in waves of terror and despair
A look, a scowl, the hip laden hand,
Fingers pointed, icicles in our hearts,
Crushing and freezing, choking the light and power from us.

The faces of condemnation chilled the fire in our gut.
And limp and lame became our energetic signature
As the power leaked out of us and into the shadows
Paranoid and desperate our Spirit crawled

Like a wounded tiger now to be caged, tamed,
destroyed, beaten into submission.

The light slowly dimmed, our gut slowly emptied
Of this volcanic fire which we once knew.

With innocence and power gone,
This life was now a battle, an endless war, raging to survive,
Threatened at every turn with eyes searching,
agonised, looking for danger
Longing for safety,
Dreaming of arms that would hold and love us.

But we were deluded.
To be loved would not fill us with power.
To be safe is not to be vital and Spirited, living
on the wave of this vortex of power.
A ship in the harbour is safe,
But its nature, its purpose, is not lived when hiding there.

And now a life is happening,
With all of the admonitions, injunctions,
threats, damnations and critiques,

Deeply embedded in the psyche, in the Soul.
Off we wander into a world where threat
lurks, skulks and hovers,
Waiting to pounce.

You see a child in the street, open and
undefended, smiling and laughing
Greeting strangers as though all are friends.
And the parents walking behind – faces hard and calcified,
Threatened and suspicious, contracted and cautious
Not living life … surviving life.
Is this what has become of us? Is this our destiny?

Angry, contracted, a subtle, bitter,
paranoia colouring every word,
Until we feel safe, until there is no danger.
But life is dangerous.
There is always death.
Everywhere there is life and death.
But death terrifies us.
Death is to be avoided, never discussed, never faced.
It is the end and we are addicted to beginnings, to birth.

And so every time the mind asks: "Will I be
late, early, will I upset you, hurt you,
Be seen as selfish, bad, a money grubber,
manipulative, far left, far right, too in the middle?"
Our power is gone,
Lost on the last light of the Westward setting sun.

And the mind makes its greatest mistake,
It tries to stop what just happened, to undo what is done.
The craziness of it, the insanity every day, hundreds of
times, waiting, waiting, waiting for accidents, mistakes,
tragedy, disaster, around which corner will they come?
The beady, anxious slit-eyed-anxiety,
anticipating hurt, pain, sadness, loss,

This never ending, winding road that leads to fear's door,
Will it ever disappear?

Will I make enough money, will I get sick, will my partner die,
When will I die, am I in the best place
possible, with just the right person,
Doing just the right thing?
Am I have serving well or enough,
Am I creating a legacy?
And the greatest, the ultimate question:
Am I living an authentic life, true to my
nature, my core, my essence?

And the best way to do this is to remember the fire,
To take heat to those embers in your gut,
And to fan them with the winds of light,
The winds of courage, the winds of memories
Long gone, where Power once was,
So natural.

So you notice your mind having fearful thoughts,
And so quickly, ever so quickly, the body responds,
Contracts and tightens, leeks its power outwards
Into space.
And yet the endless doing of this insanity.
In this moment all is lost, a stuckness,
Jammed stock still into the solid frozen ground of your being.
How to change the past?
What a fruitless virtual exercise in madness.

But there is a cure.
To just notice the thought and the feeling arising
And to keep noticing and to watch the energy of Spirit
Rising equally to meet and hold in the
palm of its metaphorical hand
The hurt the pain the suffering and the anxiety.
And slowly this pain begins to take on a

different hue, a different patina,
As spirit in its all-encompassing endless loving being,
Allows what is to be
And simultaneously transforms it.

Leaving love and power in its wake.

And so ... slowly we remember what
this power in our gut feels like
The energy returns, this primitive, primordial and vital flame
Awakens and burns, burns with a heat that is fire awakening
And the oxygen that feeds it comes from a heart and a mind
That no longer fears destruction and death
Free of the enslaved conditioned laws, fashioned in
The forgery of the pain of our teachers.

Life and death are honoured equally
This body is here and is already gone
Transient and beautiful is this world of form
Spirit's home ... for now.

A gigantic tidal wave of power floods outward
From the centre of your gut into every cell of your body.
Forged-heat-power returned.
At last.
Solid as granite, but alive, pulsating, throbbing with LIFE!
Power awakening, dancing and rejoicing in its return,
To its home.
We enter the Gateway, we salute our God nature,
We see it in everything around us and we
Dance, delighted, expanded, whole and complete
Amidst the beauty of transient imperfection,
That is this world,
This planet,
This earth,
Our home.

Mark Peter Kahn.

CHAPTER 14

What Would it Feel Like if...?

The technique for this section is contained in the theoretical description.

THE ANSWER IS IN THE BODY

Living inside a monkey-mind-dancing from tree to tree
I'm giddy with words and thoughts and pictures
First this way, then that way then the
other way and then back again
What a rollercoaster, tormented and endless journey
This mind, this thinking machine.

Every answer has 1,000 tributaries
Each answer breeds another question.
I'm in two minds, three minds, four minds
About this and that and the next thing.
Medusa, sprouting endless stories of confusion and pain.

And then, slowly the stopping of this listening to the mind.

I listen for the answer in my body
This genius mechanism awake and alight
With instinct and intuition.

What would it feel like to listen to this genius?
Below the neck
A subtle vibrant, beautiful energy

Pure truth, just knowing.

What would it feel like...
To dissolve into my true nature?
The answer, wordless, energetic, poetry from the body
Speaking in a language beyond words and concepts.

Like a flower opening, like the waves breaking
upon the coarse white sand,
Crystal pure
Truth.

Mark Peter Kahn.

By now you know the phrase "Nothing can exist without two sides" rather well, which really means that, no matter how hard you try, there will always be negatives in your life. Everything that emerges into your experience is going to have negatives and positives. Everything!

I often joke that if a journalist asked me for a five-second summary to the question "What creates the biggest problem for human beings on this planet?", my answer would be:

"Our fantasies that we can get rid of the negative!"

And so the method presented in this book is not without negatives. And the biggest negative is that the techniques are very much a *doing* process. Now you might think I'm crazy criticising my own technique.

Well I don't think so.

I just want to be honest with you and to alert you to the inherent drawback of this technique, as there are drawbacks to every single technique you've ever worked with.

In essence, *doing* can become very tiring. One is always having to be making something happen, bringing in the power or the love or whatever it is.

So the technique presented in this chapter is the antidote to the potentially tiring process of always doing.

In addition, it is just a beautiful method, designed to get you to love and power with ease and simplicity.

It is called: "What would it feel like if…?" (Wwifli…?).

This is not a normal question.

Normally when we ask ourselves questions or when someone else asks us a question we are looking for the answer in the *mind*. This is useful, practical and simply a part of everyday living.

In this process we are doing something very different; we are asking the *body* a question. So, for example, you might ask:

"What would it feel like if I had no resistance to this irritating person?"

If you asked the mind this question, the mind would speculate and come up with all sorts of possibilities and the energy would be locked into the mind, into the head. In addition, the mind would get defensive and say things such as, "But they *are* irritating and so it's logical to have resistance to being irritated, isn't it?"

But can you begin to picture what it would feel like if you ignored the mind completely, which is what I want you to do? Simply ask the question and notice what the answer is *in the body*.

Many people really freak out when I ask them not to access their mind when I ask this question, because they are so habituated to referencing their minds!

To help you to do this, I want you to notice that there are many times in our lives when our body does give us answers to questions. It does this, in fact, without us having to ask it.

Just picture yourself eating a meal. At some point in the process your body will say I've eaten enough.

How do you know this?

You don't know how you know it, but you just know that your body doesn't want you to put another piece of food in its mouth. Now some people are better at listening to this kind of response from the body than others, but nevertheless the body does know when it has had enough to eat.

The people who struggle to do this are people who have dieted and starved themselves into oblivion. So, if this is you, then here are some more examples.

You meet a new person, with whom there is business potential. They seem to have all the credentials and seem to be just right for this new association, but you have a feeling in your gut about them, something isn't right.

That gut feel is saying: "Be careful, you can't trust this person."

Now the mind can give all sorts of reasons why you have this problematic "gut feel", but that isn't the point here. The point is you have a sense that this person is dubious and the mind isn't the first place that this dubiousness begins.

It is in the gut.

And there is lovely expression, which says: "You can be in two minds about something, but not in two stomachs."

In other words, listening to our gut feel can be very helpful because it is clear, unequivocal and not filled with "on the one hand, on the other hand, but I'm wondering..."

How many times in your life have you listened to a piece of music and your body just moves into this magnificent expansion and openness? Your body has answered the question "Do I like this piece of music?" before the mind has a chance to even begin to think about it, or at least simultaneously to the mind's comments. Often we experience it as an opening in the heart.

Of course, our heart is closing down multiple times a day to all sorts of situations which we don't like. If you are sensitive to conflict, your body – your heart and gut – responds the moment it hears the conflictual tone of voice from the other person, that threatening look on their face, in their eyes.

Our bodies are highly sensitive instruments opening and closing hundreds of times a day, saying "yes" and "no" to situations we like and love or resist and hate. We know that this is happening all the time, but we just don't pay too much attention to it because we are so fixated on our minds. Mr Descartes returns to mind once again.

But you are not just your thoughts. Your feelings and sensations and intuitions are as important, and sometimes more important, than your thinking, not to speak of Spirit, Soul, Pure Consciousness, Awareness.

So let's go back to our question: "What would it feel like if I had no resistance to this irritating person?"

Just picture that person and notice the response from your body. There is a whole range of responses that people have when this process is working and all of them are in the same kind of category. There is an opening, an expansiveness, a relaxing, a stillness, a sense of calming down and the dissolving of the resistance. Which is what the technique is about. It's helping you to get into the space where the intelligence of the body enables the resistance to dissolve.

Of course, not everybody has this opening and calming down in response to the question. Many people contract even further or just stay the same.

So the thing to do here is to ask the question, feel the contraction remaining the same or being slightly reduced but still being there, and then what you do is:

Feel the contraction and allow it to deepen and stay with it!

This is a very important step. You cannot try to force the dissolving of the negative emotion; you need to simply welcome and allow it to be there and then go back to the "What would it feel like" question.

The other thing you can do is re-phrase the question. I'll get to that.

You might also want to use *Cultivating Wisdom* to dissolve the beliefs that are preventing you from allowing yourself to dissolve and release the negative emotion.

For some people this takes a bit of practice, so you need to be patient with yourself. You cannot force this process; it is a listening process. You need to learn to listen to your body, to notice how the body is responding to everything it sees and hears and feels and tastes and touches.

To help you to get better at this you want to go about your day simply noticing your body's answer to various questions. You walk into a meeting. Notice how your body responds to the energetic signature in the room. Just notice very simply if it is closed or open. Notice to whom your heart opens or closes. Just think about your email inbox and the question "Do I want to approach my emails?"

So as you notice your resistance for instance to your email inbox, just ask yourself the question "What would it feel like if I had no resistance to my inbox?", and see if there is an expansion in the body, a softening towards doing emails.

In essence, this process is asking the body a question, which spontaneously enables the body to dissolve the negative energetic signature arising from a situation. The body wants to heal. The body wants to help us to heal. The body is very good at healing.

Just think about all of the times when you've cut yourself, or hurt yourself, or injured yourself. The body is very good at healing itself and you don't have to go about your day checking if the healing is happening.

As I'm typing, I'm noticing a wanting to get this book finished. So I stop typing and noticed how this "wanting" reflects a fantasy that having the book finished would be better than having it unfinished – which is the kind of thing we spend our lives doing, yes?

And so I simply ask myself the question:

"What would it feel like if this moment of typing an unfinished book was perfect, no worse than having a complete and published book?"

And the Stillness emerges.

So what I want to do now is give you some examples of the kinds of Wwifli... questions that you can ask your body. I suggest that you read through the list fairly quickly and asterisk those items that evoke an immediate resonance in you and then come back again to those that don't at a later time. Work with the asterisked ones on a daily basis and as you go about your day just notice when you have a resistance to someone or something and ask yourself the question Wwifli...?

Learn to create your own questions too!

WHAT TO DO IF IT DOESN'T WORK?

Just one more thing before we get to the questions.

Sometimes asking the question for the first time doesn't work.

So I'm working with a man whose wife has cheated on him and I ask him: "What would it feel like to forgive her?" And he just completely shuts down. The pain is so overwhelming that he just cannot do it.

So I rephrase the question: "What would it feel like to let go of all of the feelings and thoughts about the affair?" And it starts to work. We come back to the first question later.

So work with and practise finding different ways of phrasing the question and that should help you.

Use this method for any belief system you have that creates pain in you or any painful emotion. I suggest you ask the question a number of times before exploring my explanation, so that you get the energetic signature of the process before you start to use the mind to understand it.

I have given descriptions as to the underlying meanings of the issue but I suggest that you do the process before reading the descriptions, because the descriptions are intellectual. When you have read the descriptions then go back and do the process again and notice if anything changes.

THE WWIFLI QUESTIONS

What would it feel like to drop the fantasy that controlling life will make me happy?

Most of us live in the mythical world where we wish and/or believe that we could control everything that happens. And so as soon as something happens that we don't like, we contract internally, and try to change it, and all we do is create suffering for ourselves.

What would it feel like to not rate, or score, or compare myself to anything or anyone?

The rating systems of life are immense and deeply embedded. To begin to stop dropping this rating system is to free yourself of the prison of competitive conditioning.

What would it feel like to believe that I was magnificent, before approval and success?

This is the essence of Original Self-Esteem and to rest in this place is uplifting to say the least. Just look at the spontaneous and delightful energy of a child. Can you see that you have given away this beautiful energy?

What would it feel like to have immense, unshakable Power?

Few people are aware of the degree to which they allow themselves to be disempowered by internal experiences – headaches, sickness, tiredness – and external experiences – insults, aggression, disrespect, governments and global warming. To have unshakeable Power is to be immune to these issues.

If you really feel this power as you ask the question, pause for a few minutes and feel the power in your solar plexus and allow it to expand and grow and then think of a situation or person that scares you and notice if the power diminishes, then ask the question again and see if it can expand. Spend some time doing this throughout the day.

What would it feel like to let go of all past pain?

We learn to repress and deny and ignore the pain from the past, but it impacts us unconsciously. Watch what happens as you begin to dissolve it.

What would it feel like to really, really, really live in the moment?

As long as you are living in the mind, connected to and identified with your thoughts, you cannot be in the present moment. The present moment is just being, it is not about thinking. So the more that you can simply let go of the content of mind and just be experiencing life, the more energised and powerful and loving you are going to feel.

What would it feel like if I had the innocence and stillness of my cat, or dog?

Innocence is outside of mind, free of the prison of judgement and evaluation and conditioning. Look at your cat or dog. Look into their eyes. Can you feel that innocence in them, in you?

What would it feel like if I stopped trying to fight my life?

We think that all of the pain in life comes from the problems in life. So don't take my word for it. Just notice what happens and how you feel when you stop trying to fight and resist life and see if life suddenly becomes more okay. If it does, then the problem isn't with life, it's in your resistance to it.

What it would it feel like if I stopped trying to control everyone and everything?

It's such a laughable paradox. We are trying to control everything in order to be happier and we are not seeing that in the releasing of control, happiness emerges internally!

There is the most exquisite Jeff Foster quote: "Nothing can make you happy, Until nothing can make you happy." Stop looking on the outside and relate to the world from the happiness that you *are!*

What would it feel like to know that I was not my thoughts?

This is the most powerful freedom-enhancing thing you can do. It is our thoughts that are the prison in which pain is created. There is a beautiful comment made by Jim Carrey In a speech to college graduates. He said: "The peace that we're after lies somewhere beyond personality." And the personality is created in the mind.

Most people need to do quite a bit of meditative work to get this because the addiction and identification with thoughts is so powerful.

What would it feel like to know that I could experience perfect health?

We are so often desperately struggling to be more healthy and doing affirmations around our health when, in fact, what's going on is that we are not truly believing that we can experience great health. So you are really working with your belief systems here.

What would it feel like to dissolve the incessant wanting and not wanting in my life?

This is very similar to the dissolution of "fantasies" process I mentioned earlier. To be outside of wanting and not wanting is to be the love that you are that doesn't want anything else in order to feel happier.

What would it feel like if I didn't treat everything I had to do as an emergency?

One of the greatest problems with stress is that we turn things that aren't emergencies into emergencies. If you are a very reliable and responsible person this is a very powerful process.

What would it feel like to dissolve into the energy of trust now?

Trust is available for us at any point in time. To simply trust that all is good, that all is well is a most beautiful energy.

What would it feel like to know totally that trust was my true nature?

If you knew that beneath all desire was trust and truth, they would be a great surrender into Peace.

What would it feel like to dissolve into my true nature?

Can you feel that your true nature is resting and waiting beneath all of the chaos of the mind and the stories that we create?

What would it feel like to know that trust was my energetic signature across all lifetimes?

Perhaps we do get reincarnated and have many lifetimes. If you could feel this energetic signature of trust, across all times, past present and future, how wonderful.

What would it feel like if I was free of the conditioned rules of my culture?

This is immensely important and very powerful. Just about every time you feel anxiety and guilt, you're susceptible to your conditioning. Kids of one or two years old do not experience guilt naturally or spontaneously. They have to be taught how to feel guilty. So every moment that you feel guilt it is something that has been brainwashed into you. Do you want to go on living like this?

What would it feel like to allow life … to live me rather than trying to live my life?

In the meditation process I will share with you later, the basis of it is *just sitting, doing nothing.* You connect with the energy that is not trying to create and contrive experience. You begin to discover that doing happens without the mind trying to make it happen, without the mind trying to *do* it. You are dumping the conditioned rule given to us by René Descartes and this culture. As long as you think you are the mind and you are the doer, you are a slave to Mr Descartes.

What would it feel like if the mind was a tool through which life was lived?

To continue to use the mind in all of its magnificence but to be able to let go of it when you're trying to manage feelings and control the world is to have the mind in its true place. Trying to use the mind to do something that it was not designed to do is like trying to get your motorcar to fly!

LOVE

I want to talk a little more about love. Love is the foundation of Self-Esteem. If we truly, truly love ourselves, then our Self-Esteem will be immense, although it might lack some power.

So I want to return to the statement I made in the introduction:

Can I love myself now, for no reason at all?

What I actually want you to do is ask yourself: "What would it feel like to love myself now, for no reason?"

Just notice what comes up. Many people have this immense contraction and resistance and confusion that comes up, and the reason for this is that because we are so immersed in Acquired Self-Esteem, it seems preposterous and insane to think of loving oneself for *no reason.*

So I recommend that you picture yourself as baby, one year old, and ask yourself if you can feel love for this baby. Looking at a photograph can assist in this process.

Can you slowly begin to be able to just feel great love for yourself as a baby?

And then ask yourself if you can feel the sense of "being-ness" that that baby has, that indefinable something that makes that baby so lovable, and then to feel that that "being-ness" is right here, right now.

It's in you as an adult sitting here despite all of the psychological noise and judgements that seem to overwhelm it.

And slowly, slowly, you can begin to feel the love that you are and the love for yourself as you are, right here, right now.

You cannot rush this process because you're reversing all of the conditioning of Acquired Self-Esteem, which says you have to **do** something to be lovable, or be something or somebody in order to be lovable.

Once you can do this, the next question arises:

> *What would it feel like to love myself in the face of intense rejection from others?*

Loving one-self in the face of intense rejection is really the ultimate test. Most people need to work with this many times over in order to truly get the energy that this enables. Why do I say energy?

Because to allow the criticisms and rejections of others to determine our identity is immensely draining to the system. It drains our energy.

CHAPTER 15

From Fear to Trust.

BEYOND FEAR IS TRUST

I am the Victim.
Empty inside. No trust no faith in this
That I am.
All around me is danger
So I feed the fearful thoughts
As truth,
Hoping that this will give me power.

I manage, arrange, master this world this life
Digging for water where I see a shimmering mirage.
To no avail, pointless, wandering in circles in a
dry caked desert scorched burned, lifeless.

Just to see that trust in this that I am is the energy of life.
Trust calms the mind, opens the heart, awakens my Spirit
To drift on the wind as a cloud
To float as destiny prescribes.

Mark Peter Kahn.

For years I have heard people say, "Love is the opposite of fear."
I just didn't get it, it didn't resonate for me.

And then one day I was working with a client who had this immense resentment that her organisation, which up until then had been offering flexitime, was now insisting that people clock in and out of work. Not only was she angry, but she also had a sadness and a fear sitting underneath it. This is what emerged from our discussion.

She had always longed to be understood and recognised for her diligence and reliability and commitment to work, and relationships. When this wasn't appreciated she would feel hurt, sad and resentful and then most importantly she had this anxiety that she would be reprimanded if she wasn't seen as good, and this fear was then turned into anger when she wasn't recognised.

And suddenly it dawned on me. Trust is the opposite of fear. Not trust in the normal sense of the word. Normally what we understand by trust is: "I can trust you to care about me or not betray me or be on time or be reliable." This is an expectation that we have of the world and when we trust the world we expect our desires to be fulfilled by the world, to be mirrored by the world. I'm talking about a different kind of trust here.

I am talking about a trust which says if I'm reliable and you don't recognise and appreciate that, then I trust that I can deal with it, that I can appreciate myself and value myself enough to not be upset by the fact that you are critical and are rejecting of me. Trust is saying: "I can handle anything, especially when things go badly."

"I trust that I have enough power and sense of self that I don't need to manipulate the world in order to feel good."

"I am enough."

"I am worthy and special and if you don't recognise what I am, that has nothing to do with me."

When anxiety emerges in me and I fear failure, misfortune, trouble ... trust says:

"I trust myself. I trust that life is the way it is with all of its imperfections and neurosis. It's okay, I'm okay. All is well, even if it's not well!"

Trust is *having the energetic signature* of looseness, openness, surrender to what is, allowing what is to unfold.

"All things are unfolding in perfect time."

What does this mean?

It means that as you have a thought to do something, say a piece of work, you are excited about it – and often with excitement comes anxiety – and you start to contract anxiously into wanting to get this thing done and all of the anxious thoughts that go with it:

• "Will I get this done perfectly?"

• "Will I get this done as I want it to be done?"

• "Will I forget this wonderful new thought?"

• "Can I put this together on paper as beautifully as it feels in my head?"

• "I must control this to get the best possible outcome."

All of these contracted thoughts are fear.

The energy of fear is the opposite of trust. Why?

Because trust is not having any of these thoughts, and trust is most particularly a *feeling* and a *sensation,* which is experienced as a vast, infinite stillness, calmness, expansiveness, which is completely in the now, in the present.

It is the energetic signature of Original Self-Esteem. Doing is happening but it is inspired. It does not have the contracted tension of desperate wanting.

This is a very beautiful place.

This energetic signature of trust heals the energy of fear.

Fear is the opposite of this because fear is saying I have to manipulate you and the world in order to feel okay. We live in fear because we don't believe that we can handle the next thing and the next thing and the next thing. Trust is the opposite. Trust is saying I don't mind what the next thing is, I have so much power and love and innocence inside of me that I can deal with the next thing.

So you fear being late for a meeting. Trust says: "I can handle being late. I can handle the consequences, your anger, or the problems being late causes."

"Trust dissolves fear."

I've always been fascinated with my cats who will go into a cupboard or a door that is open without considering whether they have a way out. That innocence is trust. That innocence doesn't need to be sure it has a getaway strategy.

Our lives are filled with getaway strategies.

If you do this then, I'll do that.

If the world does this, then I'll do that.

And so we are endlessly creating stories in our heads in order to make sure that we are safe, just in case.

I'm not saying *never* have a getaway strategy, a plan B!

But we overdo it.

We overdo it monumentally!

I am endlessly assailed by phone calls from companies that want to sell me more and more and more insurance.

Today my insurance company wanted to sell me insurance to lower the write-off value of my car. So they supposedly want to give me more freedom if my car gets damaged, by lowering the write-off value from 70% to 40%.

It's absurd. I smiled when the salesperson gave me his story. I told him that by buying the insurance, I would be investing in my fear. After some discussion, he finally got the message.

Or so it seemed.

Obviously I have the basics: insurance for my home, my car and medical aid. But all of the other calls to insure everything I do is capitalising on my fear, my lack of trust in my ability to manage the vicissitudes of life.

Trust is saying I have the power and capacity to manage all of the ups and downs, the pleasures and the pains, the uncertainties of life.

Trust is the ultimate in Self-Esteem, because it is saying, "I am enough as I am."

If you do not believe that you are enough, that you have the love and the power and the resources within you to deal with life then you cannot trust yourself to deal with difficulties as they emerge and you try to manipulate and control people and events, in order to feel okay.

And so, in this work, one's focus moves away from, can I trust you, or the world, to:

"Can I trust myself?"

Can I believe enough in the power of myself to be calm and still and open and innocent and loving?

And so we get to the next level of this issue. Our lives are spent incessantly doing things. We do things often because we are inspired, but then it becomes a "doing" in order to gain Self-Esteem or gain control or feel a sense of accomplishment or to get appreciation and approval and love from the world. And so the doing becomes a manoeuvring and a manipulation which has the energetic signature of *desperation* in it.

Thoreau said that we live lives of "quiet desperation". I think it's true and we're desperately manoeuvring and doing and fixing and trying to get love externally because we don't trust ourselves. This reflects an emptiness inside which we are running from and so we cannot allow behaviour to flow from a *fullness* inside of us.

Action that comes from emptiness leads to chaos and disaster. If your partner behaves in a way that leaves you feeling anxious and unloved and empty inside, your responses are going to be neurotic and it is going to create conflict with them.

Isn't this what much of life is about?

People are so obsessed with the fact that there is war in the world, but look at the war inside of us, from which comes an attempt to gain peace from the outside.

And so we make war with the outside because there is war on the inside. I read this beautiful quote from little girl named Lara, aged seven, in a magazine.

She said:

"People will never stop fighting wars, they can't even get on in blocks of flats!"

Perfect – beautiful.

Can you go inside, into the emptiness and discover that there is a fullness there and all you need, is inside of you?

If you fear your partner dying or leaving you, there is no trust. Trust says: "It may hurt, it may be painful, but I trust that I can be okay with the pain and I will be filled enough with love to dissolve the pain."

I see so many people go from cynicism about relationships, to romanticism.

Back and forth, bi-polar. They don't know that in the middle is balance.

Cynicism says: "Love ... shmuv, it doesn't exist."

But this is the love of fantasies. It's the love without imperfection. It's not real. It's not life.

Then this person meets someone and falls "in love" and they think it's perfect.

Now they are enchanted – romantic. But it's not real. It's exaggerated perfection. And they have to be let down, and when they are, they swing back to cynicism. What an awful way to live. And it's deeply superficial.

When we are outside of the present moment we are not trusting that all will be well and that even if it's not well, that's fine.

Straining desperately while you're making the coffee because you want to get to that piece of work that isn't finished yet is not trusting that which is inside of you.

Trust says that the capacity to unfold that piece of work and that how it unfolds will be fine.

So the straining and the stressing and the escaping from the present moment is really a *lack of trust in oneself and one's ability to allow life to unfold as it will!*

You might ask, what is that we are trusting? We are trusting our Spirit or Pure Consciousness or Soul, our primary nature.

The mind thinks it is in control of our life. We think we are our thoughts, we think we are our minds.

I have described to you how Original Self-Esteem is about flowing with an energy and power and love that is unselfconscious. Trust only emerges when we dissolve our self-consciousness. The mind is immensely self-conscious. It is always splitting itself into parts and thinking about itself and pondering and ruminating and commentating on creating stories about itself and life.

And it thinks that if it stops doing this, it will fall apart.

This is a sandwich-board thought.

It's a lie.

So the way to test the lie is to discover that your heart beats now and your digestive system and immune system and your eyes and your kidneys and your liver are all functioning now without you having to think about them. What's doing that? You might argue that it's a bunch of neurons and chemicals in the brain doing it. It's very difficult issue to argue.

My sense is that Consciousness is doing it and that often our behaviour is the same. When we are outside of self-consciousness we just flow, and trust is what is functioning at that point. We don't need to second-guess ourselves. We just live as we are, magnificent, flowing, energised and powerful.

What does it mean to love yourself?

I had the most fascinating experience yesterday. I had a whole lot of errands to do around lunchtime and was getting pretty exhausted – you know this chronic fatigue thing – and I'm trying to get out of my local shopping centre and there is a long queue of traffic. And when I'm getting near the exit, I see an option for me to get into a second lane to escape the traffic because I'm going to be turning right at a circle, at the exit to the shopping centre, and the backed up traffic is going left at the circle.

The guy in front of me has the front end of his car sticking into this optional second lane that I want to create and I start to get frustrated. My frustration is exaggerated by my exhaustion and I become angry because he's blocking my path to home and my bed.

He looks at me and I gesture to him to move out of the way. He rolls down his window and starts speaking.

So I edge forward, rolling down my window and ask him why he can't move out of the way, and he says to me, in a really kind and reasonable way: "You look like you are shouting. I'm wondering why you are shouting?"

And shouting, I reply: "You're blocking my path to turn right at the circle and you're going left!"

The traffic moves forward and I manage to squeeze through and turn right out of the traffic circle.

And I notice that I'm judging myself for being angry at this very reasonable guy.

And now the work begins.

Can I simply love my anger?

Simply love the fact that I am just purely and simply angry? There could be many other reasons for my anger. Maybe I had received bad news and I was upset ... whatever.

Being able to love myself in the moment, not just for no reason, *but in the face of good reasons not to,* is a beautiful thing to do.

It is very powerful to learn to just honour your anger *in the moment of being angry!*

Not justifying it or explaining it, but simply honouring the fact that that's what you are doing and feeling and you cannot be doing anything different because that's what you're doing right now.

What's really beautiful about this is that to love yourself and give yourself the freedom to be angry means you can give other people the freedom to be angry at you, because how often have you judged the anger of others, and it's partly a projection, because you are judging the anger in yourself.

And so when you are doing "Trust", you trust that all of your emotions and the emotions of others are fine, it's okay, all is well as it is, rather than "Life should be different from the way it is".

Go to Chapter 26 for the strategy.

PART TWO
The Strategies

When working with these techniques it is very important to realise that most people have an expectation that their progress will be a straight line graph upwards. I've never seen it happen. It looks like this: progress, setback, progress, setback, progress ... on and on. If you realise this, you won't get deflated and give up.

In addition, when you have a setback you will often think you are back at square one. This is rarely the case, but it may feel like that.

So if you know this, you can be prepared.

In addition, don't expect these techniques to always work well when you are sick or tired or very depressed. Remembering this will prevent you from giving up.

Success in anything is determined to a significant degree by your ability to persist and not give up.

A cautionary note. Do not expect these methods to work every time. Nothing works every time! The more you practise them, the better you will get. The clients that I've worked with over the years, who've practised five times a day, as situations crop up in their lives, do the best.

Many years ago, I consulted a Barbara Brennan healer to help me with my fatigue issue. The work we did together was really helpful. She left town. I recently found another Brennan healer in New Mexico in the U.S. Her name is Nina Twombly. We have started working together via Skype. She is awesome.

I would like to recommend that you do this healing work with her. It will significantly deepen your capacity to use these techniques, accessing love and power in the body.

nina@ninatwombly.com

CHAPTER 16

Activating Love for No Reason

These techniques are immensely powerful, if you are prepared to give them time and attention. I hope you enjoy them.

A MEDITATION

The meditation aspect of this process is adapted from Adyashanti

JUST SITTING - DOING NOTHING

When doing is released into earth and sky
Into nebula far beyond our spinning world
When the striving, pushing, driving,
controlling mind-seeking game
Is just allowed to be.

The utter unspeakable Just Sitting
So pure and simple
Comes to rest like a cat silently curled in innocence.
The beauty of her grace
The home longed for

Always here
Hidden in the sacred darkness
Arises to express the ineffable joy
Of emptiness beyond word or thought.

Mark Peter Kahn.

AUDIO RECORDINGS

There are six meditations in this section. The written text is in this book. However, I have made audio recordings of them, as listening to them is the best way to get maximum benefit. I recommend that you listen to the recordings, in addition to reading them. All of the italicised sections have been recorded.

You can access an audio recording of this meditation. If you're reading this as an eBook, you can click on the link below to access the recording. If you are reading this on a hardcopy, type the link into your web browser to access the audio.

http://bit.ly/poemsmeditations

You are now going to slow down and calm down, in order to firstly, learn how to really slow down into a deep Stillness and then secondly, to use the energy of this Stillness to learn to love yourself for no reason.

You will then learn to access internal power and use love and power to dissolve negative emotions.

Sit down. Close your eyes. Simply do nothing. Can you notice what it feels like to simply sit and do nothing? This is very unusual. For most of our lives we are running around doing something. We have endless "agendas". Engaging in activities and trying to get outcomes, achieve a result, reach an objective, connecting with our goals. Right now you are doing nothing; you are just sitting, with no objective in mind.

It might seem strange, odd. It is. Just simply sit and do nothing. I am giving you permission to do nothing. Not only that, **I am recommending it**. *Just notice what it feels like to do nothing at all. Simply sitting.*

The mind might start racing around trying to get a hold of something to do, to wrap itself around an object, an activity, a goal. To question this process, to run from this process.

If this happens, then just watch the mind. Smile gently at the mind that is incessantly active and always looking to do something. It even wants to do something with nothing! I am now smiling at this. What a "doing" culture we have created. Nothing wrong with that – in fact, it is wonderful, it has many benefits. But what you want to be able to do is de-activate the doing. And that is what is happening now.

This is not the time for doing. This is the time for not doing.

So ... there are two things happening here.

You are just sitting doing nothing and then allowing the mind just to be as it is. Not trying to control it, not trying to interfere with its incessant ruminating and rambling and trying to fix and do and make something happen.

It is the "doing" that distracts us, that prevents us from achieving peace. Indeed, most meditations involve a very powerful "doing". The doing is aimed at achieving peace.

What you might begin to notice is that when you stop doing, Peace spontaneously arises. Can you let go even more deeply of any doing and attempts at manipulating this process right now and simply notice that the more you do nothing, the more the peace arises.

If the Stillness or sense of Presence does not arise, then continue to do nothing until it does. It will.

In order to work with the emotions, you need to have a sense of this Stillness or Presence there. It is the container, the support for you to then start working with the emotions.

Just sitting ... doing nothing ... this is the meditation. Notice what happens when you engage in ... not doing.

So now, hopefully you have some sense of Stillness or Presence arising inside of you. Only continue with this exercise once there is some sense of Stillness there. You do not need to have this Stillness exclusively; it can be accompanied by any emotions or thoughts.

Now I want you to picture a dog or a cat or a very small child whom you love. It is best to work with animals or small children because we have less complicated relationships with them. However, if you cannot do this, then picture a person whom you love now or loved in the past, with whom you did not have a particularly complicated relationship.

Now picture being with them and feeling the love that you get or got from them. And you are loving them and they are loving you, and fill yourself with this energy of being loved. Fill yourself with this energy and allow it to expand and grow and expand throughout every part of your body, into every cell of your being.

You might feel it particularly in your heart centre, in the middle of your chest. Simply allow this energy to grow and expand and resonate as deeply as you can. Do this for a few minutes. Stop for a few minutes, as you allow this love to expand inside of you...

Now I want you want to let go of the picture of the animal or the baby or the other person and simply feel yourself sitting here filled with love, energised and awake and alive.

You might find that letting go of the animal or the person leads to the love reducing. Go back to the animal or person and re-energise yourself with this love and then let go of them.

You are training yourself here to connect more and more deeply with love, for no reason, Original Self-Esteem, without connection to anything or anyone else.

You want to practise filling yourself with love 10 or 15 or 20 times a day. The more you do this, the more powerful it will become. Most of the focus in our culture is on learning to love others more and be a better person. The reason this needs quite a bit of work is that you've probably spent very little time in your life actively loving yourself.

Can you now take a few moments to think of a special person in your life? Can you love them for no reason? If you are worthy of this love, can you now see that they are worthy of love for no reason, too. Notice if there are any beliefs obstructing you doing this and dissolve them. Perhaps they have hurt you or been unkind. Dissolve these reasons in love and love them for no reason. Now choose another two or three people in your life and do the same with them...

Now choose somebody who has rejected you or hurt you recently or in the past. Can you love them for no reason? This is very, very liberating because our rejection of others is a prison for us. It is a prison of resentment and hurt and pain and a desire for revenge and wanting to change them.

Everyone is doing their best, even when they're not doing their best. Can you love the whole world for no reason?

In a moment you are going to open your eyes. When you do this **stay with the Stillness**. *This is very important. Usually when we do closed-eye relaxation or meditation, as soon as we open our eyes we jump back into an over-aroused state. You want to learn to start living your life more and more from this state of Stillness. So now, you can open your eyes and just look around – from the Stillness, through the Stillness. Notice how different this feels.*

When you practise doing this, every time stay with the Stillness. You can begin to live from the Stillness from the love that you are.

ACTIVATING INTERNAL POWER FOR NO REASON

What is really fascinating about internal power is that many people who are overwhelmed by pain cannot find their power. So what I suggest is that you do the meditative process above and then access power.

POWER STRATEGY

- Spend 10 minutes doing the meditation "Just sitting" and then...

- Think of a time when you felt powerful, when you had a sense of self-worth, a sense of having achieved something and being special.

- Perhaps it was the first time you rode a bike, or were told you were clever, or beautiful, or you did well in some sport, or you graduated, or somebody in authority whom you admired told you that you were special.

I had a teacher when I was 12 years old, a time when I felt very fragile and vulnerable and sensitive, and he gave me a sense of being special, of having a quality about me that made me feel immensely worthwhile. I only realised many years later how important this was for me, the sense that I got from him, that I was special. When I was 45 years old I tried to contact him, to tell him how much this had meant to me. He had passed away. I felt so sad that I couldn't do this.

Can you find anyone in your past that gave you that sense that there was a specialness about you, a sense of value and of being *validated*?

- Now, expand that sense of power, that sense of validation, of specialness.

- Really expand and sit with it for two or three or four minutes.

Power is primarily based in the solar plexus.
Feel the energy there and
expand it and grow it and deepen it. When you are practising this,
you can simply feel the energy there and deepen it.

Learn to do this instantaneously!

- Listening to a piece of music you love while you do this can you deepen the sense of power.

- Then, and very importantly, let go of the situation that gave you the sense of power and just feel it independent of anything externally.

- The reason that you are doing this is that you want to connect with this energy that is Original and is not linked to any external event even though it might have emerged out of a particular situation – Acquired.

I am not saying here that you shouldn't get love from others.
I am saying that there is a source within that we ignore!

- Another reason that this is so important is that as you begin to go about your day and encounter pressurised situations, you want to be able to connect with this energy as simply being a part of you – not related and dependent on anything external.

- As you disconnect from the situation, you may lose the energy of the power. Then go back to the situation and keep doing this over the next few days or weeks until you can connect with this energy without reference to any event.

STILL STRUGGLING TO CONNECT WITH POWER?

- As I mentioned, many people believe that they cannot connect with their power because there's too much pain in the way. They are so identified with the painful Victim position that they do not believe the powerful Mastery position exists in them.

- *Believe me it does.*

- Alternatively, don't believe me – but test it, check it out, by doing the processes to see if power is really there, hidden beneath the pain.

- Remember a bad dream that you had. Everything in the dream is created by you, by your unconscious mind. Therefore every role played out in the dream is a part of you.

- Perhaps an animal or a monster was chasing you and you felt helpless and frightened. I had a client recently who said that guerrilla terrorists were chasing her. I got her to identify with and *be* the guerrilla terrorists. Feel the energy and the power of being that and notice how you start to connect with and identify with this power. If you can't connect with your power, it means that you are over-identified with being the Victim. This helps you to shift that misplaced identification and to connect with your power.

- Walk around feeling the energy of being the 'guerrilla terrorist' or whatever version you have.

ANOTHER OPTION...

- People who struggle to connect with their power have simply forgotten moments in which they felt powerful.

- Just think of a time when you were angry with somebody or disagreed vehemently about some issue.

- You may simply have been watching someone on television and have felt very critical of the way they were speaking or their points of view or even the way they were dressed. Just feel the energy and *power* in your disagreement and fill your being with that energy and then let go of that situation that gave you the sense of power and experience it.

- Practice feeling this power 20 times a day, especially going into pressure or conflict situations.

I LOVE MYSELF FOR NO REASON

ANOTHER MEDITATION

AUDIO RECORDINGS

You can access an audio recording of this meditation. If you're reading this as an eBook, you can click on the link below to access the recording. If you are reading this on a hardcopy, type the link into your web browser to access the audio.

http://bit.ly/poemsmeditations

Do a "Just sitting'" meditation for at least five or 10 minutes.

Then, can you begin to conceive of the idea that you can be pure love for no reason? Can you begin to get a sense that there is a love inside of you that is beyond the mind, beyond what others think, beyond how well you do, how successful you are, how much you are approved of in your life?

Think of a little furry rabbit. How beautiful it is, how amazing it is, how magical it is. What created that? Could we create that in the laboratory? Can we create a human body, your body, in the laboratory?

Can you look at your body and see the magnificence of it. The trillions of cells functioning in harmony to enable it to see and hear and think and feel and digest food and pump the heart and get rid of toxins and fight viruses and reflect on the meaning of life and read and strategise and plan and feel the pain of others and joy and to love others and to love yourself.

Can you look at yourself in the mirror and see an incredible creation. In this incredible creation that you are, can you feel the love that is shining there inside of you before you have done anything or not done anything said anything or not said anything?

Can you begin to encounter the magical being that is love without reason? Can you notice what it feels like, the energy and power of knowing that you are just love, just this amazing being that is love shining like the sun?

Look at a picture of yourself as an infant. Can you feel the "being-ness" of that infant? This sense of being that is there before thought, before it knows its name, its gender, before it owns things: my toothbrush, my mother, my house?

Can you feel the joy and innocence that is love shining out of that infant? Take a bit of time to do this...

Now can you notice that that "being-ness" is here right now? It has been obscured by the mind and the thoughts and the conditioning injected into you by the culture but it is here right now. Can you feel the magnificence of this energy that is pure love sitting here right now?

Notice if there are any belief systems running in your mind telling you that you cannot be love for no reason. Go through each belief system and ask: "Is this the truth?"

Common belief systems include:

*"I have to do something or be something to be lovable." Ask yourself why it is that children are lovable before they do anything? Then ask why is it that I, as an adult, should be different from this? Does love really have anything to do with **doing**?*

Can you truly feel the lie that you have to do or be something, before you are love, before you are lovable? Allow this lie to dissolve in the light of truth, as you discover the love that you always were.

Use the steps involved in Cultivating Wisdom to dismantle all of the beliefs you have around loving yourself for no reason until you can feel yourself shining, like the sun, for no reason, other than that this is your true nature.

DISSOLVING PAIN MEDITATION

AUDIO RECORDINGS

You can access an audio recording of this meditation. If you're reading this as an eBook, you can click on the link below to access the recording. If you are reading this on a hardcopy, type the link into your web browser to access the audio.

http://bit.ly/poemsmeditations

You are now going to use love to dissolve emotional pain.

Do a "Just sitting" meditation.

When you have a sense of Stillness or Presence arising inside of you, you can continue.

Welcome in the sadness, or the hurt, or the guilt, or the anxiety ... whatever the emotion is – but just one emotion at a time – that you are feeling right now or that you are remembering from the past.

And most importantly, don't choose a big one to start with! Simply allow yourself to feel it and stay with the Stillness and the feeling.

Notice the feeling in the body and feel the feeling and the sensation in your body. Emotions are experienced below the neck, so feel the feelings in your gut, in your chest in your throat, wherever they are.

Some people say to me that their feelings are in their head. They are incorrect. The thoughts about the feelings are in the head. One can have sensations in the head, but not feelings. Just see if you can find the feelings in your body and if you can't, that's fine, then just welcome the feelings and welcome the Stillness.

And now most importantly you want to return to the sense of just sitting and doing nothing. Just sitting and doing nothing with the feelings, just watching the feelings and being with feelings and notice what happens when you just sit with the feelings.

If you do this they will begin to soften and transform. Just watch the transformation and watch the mind commentating and doing stories about it and do not interfere with the mind, just let the mind be as it is.

And then return to the feelings and allow the feelings to just be as they are and be aware of the feelings in an accepting way. Usually we want to get rid of negative feelings. We are doing something different here. We are just being with them. This might seem strange and odd, especially if you have spent a lifetime trying to get rid of negative emotions, which applies to most of us.

So, you are being with the feeling of pain, or hurt or anxiety and just noticing it, not trying to manipulate it, or change it or control it. Again this is unusual. Can you notice the urge to manipulate or change or control the emotion? Smile at that desire and just be with the feeling and notice if it stays the same, gets bigger or smaller. Watch it change and allow it to change without interfering with it.

When you feel that a significant amount of pain has been dissolved, connect with the feelings of love and/or power – whichever is easiest for you – that hopefully you have been practising and allow it to surround, interpenetrate and dis-solve any feelings of pain that are still there.

If there is still pain, then watch the pain from the place of Stillness and watch it transform.

If there is still some pain left inside of you, it is probably be-cause there are belief systems that are preventing you from releasing the pain. So ask yourself, what are you believing or saying to yourself that is preventing you from dissolving the pain?

So, for example, I worked with a woman whose sister was in a lot of distress and I was helping her to dissolve her anxiety about her sister. She got stuck. I asked her if she was believing that if she didn't have anxiety, it would prevent her from car-ing and helping for her sister. She said yes, that was the case. I asked if she could picture herself without anxiety but still loving her sister and caring for her, and she said she could, and so I said perhaps the belief that you have to be anxious in order to care is a lie, and she got it and the anxiety dissolved.

The mind will create endless stories of complete nonsense that have nothing to do with the truth. You can transcend this nonsense and heal.

PARENTING FOR GREAT SELF-ESTEEM

Most parents want their kids to grow up with great Self-Esteem. The problem is that if you're a parent and your Self-Esteem isn't great then that, unfortunately, is what you are likely to pass on to your children. If you really do this work and grow your Self-Esteem, you are a gift to your kids, quite apart from how much you will be a gift to your partner and other people.

Over the years many parents have said to me: "What's the best way to talk to my kids to make them better human beings?" My reply is often: "It's not always what you say to your children as much as how you behave and what they see you doing and being that is important."

So you might tell your children that they mustn't tell lies and they must be respectful and disciplined and so on and so forth, but if they see you telling lies and being disrespectful and un-disciplined, then that's what they are likely to learn.

In addition, you might have gathered from my chapter on *Cultivating Wisdom* that to just teach your children to respect people is unskilful. You want to start learning to have dialogues with them which explore when to be respectful and when not. If somebody is manipulating you or taking advantage of you, if you treat them with too much respect, then they will walk all over you.

Of course, it gets complicated and tricky, because in situations such as this you might want to be very tough and hard on the person wanting to manipulate you, but you might also want to learn to do this in a respectful way. These are complex issues and not simply answered.

Nevertheless, what I want to share with you here is an amazing technique for working with kids, mostly up to the age of nine or 10 years old, to help them to build their Self-Esteem in the most beautiful way.

My 10-year age limit is flexible. The most important deciding factor in whether this will work or not is whether your child will let you hold them and love them. In the teenage years this gets much more difficult, especially for boys.

So your seven-year-old daughter who's been loving dancing for the last few years suddenly develops performance anxiety and doesn't want to dance anymore because the teacher is anxious about how good *she* – the teacher – looks in the eyes of the school when the kids are performing and so becomes very pushy about doing it *well.*

And your daughter says to you: "Mommy, I don't want to dance any more. I'm too scared of dancing and I want to do archery like all of my friends."

In this particular example, the mother proceeded to launch into a lecture about doing things for the joy of it and not doing things because "your friends are doing them", and she said to me: "I could just see my daughter's eyes glaze over and I had no impact on her at all." (Please note, the parental lecture is the *worst* way to communicate any learning or healing to your kids.)

"So then I remembered what you had said to me and I just held my daughter and hugged her and hugged her, and after five minutes of hugging I said to her 'Can you feel the love I am giving you inside of you?' She replied 'Yes' and then I said to her 'Now can you feel the love *melting* away all of your fear and your anxiety?'"

And after a few minutes she said: "Mommy, I feel wonderful."

This little girl went off and performed her dance routine at the centre of the stage and loved it and said afterwards that she wasn't interested in doing archery any more.

That's the process.

Here are some further guidelines in this process.

This won't work if the child doesn't want to let you hold or love them, so if they're in an angry or rebellious mood, you would need to wait for them to calm down until they are feeling softer and more vulnerable, which is connecting to the primary emotions underneath the secondary anger, and then to hug them and then melt away the negative emotions with love.

The next step that you engage involves you saying, when, for example, they are sitting some distance away from you and they say they're unhappy: "Can you feel me loving you from over here and feel the love inside of you melting away all of the hurt?"

When this works, you then teach them to start doing it when they are with their friends or apart from you at school and they are feeling hurt or sad anxious and show them how to feel love from Mom dissolving the negative emotions.

And finally what you teach them to do is to just remember the love that is inside of them has always been there, so it's no longer having to come from Mom but is generated internally, which is returning them to Original Self-Esteem.

Say: "When you are playing with the dog, there is love inside you, yes? Just remember that love. It came from you. It is always there, waiting for you to feel it."

This is a truly beautiful process and I even recommend that you picture yourself as a child in pain and take the love that you experience now back to the situation where you were a child and fill yourself with love in that situation and melt away the pain that you had then.

You can also experiment with using internal power to melt away anxiety and vulnerability and a sense of being bullied by others. Just get your kid to remember a time when they felt confident and had achieved something when they did well and you praised them and just get them to feel that feeling of internal power and use that feeling to melt away the anxiety and the vulnerability.

A BINARY ERROR

I've mentioned how parents over-use the lecture with their children. I want to elaborate on this here.

I'm working with a 37-year-old father on his anxiety and anger issues. We are talking about how hard he is on himself, how he judges and persecutes himself when he doesn't do well and doesn't achieve what he wants.

I suggest to him that he is perhaps not loving himself for no reason. He says to me that he doesn't want to become a couch potato – in other words, he is saying if he isn't hard and judge-mental on himself, then he's going to flip into passivity and non-action and achieve nothing in his life.

This is one of the most common problems I have seen in my clients in all of my years of doing this work. It's an all or nothing problem. I call it a *binary error*.

This man has a five-year-old daughter. I will call her Lucy. This is what I say to him to illustrate how the *binary error* operates and how to work with it:

"Imagine that Lucy comes home from school with her first assignment and she hasn't got a star on it. She hasn't done well. If you look at her and you say to her 'That's not very good is it?', you are teaching her self-rejection. And she is getting her first lesson in 'I'm not good enough!'

"So the best thing to say to her would be to ask how she feels and to hold her and love her and help to melt away any sense of failure or self-rejection with this love. And here's the kicker. You then say to her: 'Okay, do you want to now talk about how you can do better next time?' So you are slowly and gently moving from love and support into challenging her into growing."

The *binary error* here is that there is an assumption that there are only two options on this continuum. To push and threaten and reject on the one side and passivity or couch potato on the other. What's missing is the middle position, which is enabled by love and support and gentleness upfront, and when the trust has been built, then very slowly and gently learn to push.

Very few people, let alone parents, know how to do this, and I see this endlessly as regards the behaviour of managers and leaders in organisations.

In other words, most leaders and managers work from the same position as their parents did. Under pressure they default to coldness over professionalism, and attack.

The same issue applies to anxiety and performance. Most people believe that they need to be anxious in order to perform well. After years of exploration my conclusion is that this is complete nonsense.

The only time that anxiety is useful is if you're bored or tired, and then it can wake you up and energise you. Otherwise, everybody I've ever spoken to, including myself, does better when they're not anxious. And so the polarity of having that competitive edge because you're anxious versus passivity is just not valid. In the centre is true Original Self-Esteem.

It is balanced, powerful, energised and Still.

AN EXTRAORDINARY STORY

As regards loving yourself for no reason, I want to share with you a most extraordinary experience I had with a client yesterday. I will call her Sandra.

This is a woman with whom I've been working for some months. She is committed to her self-growth in a really deep way and has made some amazing progress. I now see her about once a month.

She walks into my office and starts crying and tells me that she is in a mess, that nothing is working and she feels terrible and she's not able to love herself and everything is falling apart.

She has problems at work, she has problems with the boyfriend, she has problems with her closest friend and that 2 kg that she is trying to lose just isn't happening.

At the end of the story she says: "I feel so helpless."

This is an extraordinary comment because she is trying so hard, too hard, to gain control to make things better and it's failing and so she feels helpless.

Adults hate feeling helpless because it reminds them of when they were three or four or five months old, helpless babies lying in a cot.

So I start to work with her, using a new concept that I've been working on for the last couple of months around helplessness – I think that this will be the subject of my next book.

Here is our dialogue:

Mark: "What I want you to do now is just notice how much you are hating the helplessness, resisting it."

Sandra: "Yes, I hate it."

Mark: "So now I want you to just feel the helplessness and surrender to it. Notice how you've been resisting the feeling of helplessness, how you have been wanting to fix things at work and with your partner and that 2 kg ... and you are feeling helpless because you are failing, trying to fix all of these things. So I want to see if you can simply surrender into the helplessness, because there's nothing you can do about it, right?"

Sandra: "Okay, I think I can do that a bit."

Mark: "Wonderful. Now I want you to see if you can really surrender a little more, notice what it feels like to surrender and notice if there is a resistance to surrendering."

Sandra: "Yes, I don't want to surrender. It feels like giving in and it feels weak."

Mark: "Yes, it does feel weak, because it scares you and because you feel like a tiny little baby, don't you?"

Sandra: "Yes I do."

Mark: "Can you see that you been trying for weeks now to fight all of these feelings of helplessness by trying to fix the things that you can't fix and you keep failing. So just for now, just for the next five minutes I you want to surrender to the helplessness, and then after the five minutes you can start resisting it again. Okay?"

Sandra: Smiling ..."Okay."

Mark: "Wonderful, and can you feel how as you smile you let go of your resistance to the helplessness, and now just surrender more and more deeply into the reality that is. Some of the greatest psychological and spiritual growth happens when we just soften into surrender. Why? Because reality wins, as Adyashanti says, "but only every time". So if we fight something – called reality – then we're going to lose, and why on earth would you want to lose?"

Sandra smiles again and her face begins to soften and I can feel the energy of softening in the room.

Mark: "So now you are just feeling the helplessness and I'm wanting to know if you can start to feel some stillness and peace arising inside of you?"

Sandra: "Yes I can. It's a relief."

(This is what happens when you surrender to helplessness. Peace arises.)

Mark: "Now can you begin to feel at least some neutrality or acceptance towards yourself as opposed to the self-rejection you've been feeling up to now?"

Sandra: "Yes, I feel neutral."

Mark: "Can you now surrender even more deeply into the helplessness, simply allow the helplessness to be there, and as you do this can you see that it is the fighting of the helplessness that is the problem, not the helplessness itself. It is not all of these problems in your life that are the problem but the fact that you are hating them and are trying to fix them and you can't fix them and that leaves you feeling helpless?"

Sandra: "Yes, I can see that and I'm starting to feel acceptance now."

Mark: "So now I want to ask you: what would it feel like to love yourself for no reason? (Please note: I am using the What would it feel like if...? Technique.) In spite of all the reasons you believe you should not love yourself, because you have work problems and relationship problems and you are trying to lose that 2 kg?"

Sandra: "Yes ... I can feel the love arising inside of me."

Mark: "Wonderful. Now can you open your eyes staying with the love that is inside of you?

"Can you see what an amazing thing has happened. We haven't changed a single thing about your life. All of the issues about your body and relationships, we haven't even talked about them, and yet you have moved from a sense of self-rejection and helplessness into just love. What this means is that it is not the problems in your life that are causing the problem in you; it is your need to control them and your resistance to the helplessness that emerges because of your wanting to control what's going on.

"Essentially we are helpless in the face of much of our wanting, and if you surrender to this helplessness, then life feels different and yes, you will begin to work with and solve some of these problems, but that'll happen in its own time and maybe now isn't the time?

"Let me ask you: for how many years have you been trying to lose 2 kg and do and then put the weight on and lose it and put it on and lose it ... endlessly?"

And Sandra smiles broadly: "Decades."

Mark: "So you are helpless in the face of the fact that you are continually trying to lose 2 kg and then you lose it and you put it on. The cycle is endless and you are helpless in the face of it. Can you surrender to the helplessness of what is happening?"

Sandra smiles and there is love in her heart and on her face for herself and for her life.

This work is just so profound, because if you really understand it, you will see that trying to fix all of the stuff on the outside is not the answer. I'm not saying you mustn't work on issue and you mustn't solve problems, but they aren't going to give you the happiness and love that you are looking for.

Happiness and love come from surrendering to the truth of what you are, which arises when you stop fighting reality.

CHAPTER 17

From Pain to Love & Power 1.0

Inside this body is pain
Deep inside every cell
Waiting to be dissolved in love
Healing is waiting, hibernating there,
Waiting for the love that you are
To enter the space.
Gentle, kind, filled with light
To hold the dis-ease and in a crucible
Of fire, to enter into a new destiny,
A metamorphosis, from caterpillar to butterfly.

See the pain that they gave you
Give it back to them – open-palmed hands
Returning suffering to the giver.

Nothing now but freedom.

Mark Peter Kahn.

Write down 15 examples of pain: i.e. hurt, rejection, grief, betrayal, helplessness, guilt, criticism, rejection, shame and trauma in your life starting as early as possible up to the present. Think about times of transition, of change, of the significant people who hurt you, rejected you and resented you. Don't write the story, just two or three words to remind you of the situation. Write down the feeling you experienced.

Examples:

"Dad said I'm stupid." – Feeling: hurt, pain.

"Mom said I'm getting fat." – Feeling: rejection, sadness.

Now go through each example and feel the pain in your body and say the thought behind the feeling.

Example:

"I'm useless."

It is very important to really *feel the pain* and make a big space for it in your body. Notice where you feel the pain. Is it in your gut, or your solar plexus a bit higher up? Is there a tightening in the throat and chest? Do the arms and legs seem to go numb or feel lame or tighten up? It is useful to feel this and experience it on a physical level. If you can't, it's absolutely fine.

When we are kids and we are attacked or criticised or abused, the shoulders and spine come forward. Often the eyes looked downwards. This is a protection mechanism that we continue to do into adulthood. When sports commentators talk about the "body language" of a team that is doing badly, this is what they are describing.

When we are praised, the spine straightens and the shoulders open. It helpful in this work if you can be aware of this process and to fully immerse yourself in the sensations, when you are opening yourself to the hurt and pain.

RECIPROCAL SWITCHING

Reciprocal Switching means to feel the pain and then go back to the love or power, then back to the pain and back to the love or power, between 30 seconds and one minute, each side. And after doing this for between three and five times, bring in the love or power to surround, interpenetrate and dissolve the pain.

Note: When you're saying these positive phrases, they are not affirmations. Affirmations are usually making a positive statement without doing any of the work in the body, in the feelings. I don't want you to say the positive phrase until you can get the positive feeling.

I did affirmations for many years and, largely speaking, they didn't help me, which is not to say that they don't help some people. But what I am saying is that many of my clients have had the same experience with affirmations as I have had.

I think that affirmations probably help about 10% of people. One of the main reasons for this is that if you can't make a connection with yourself at a physical or sensory or emotional level, the affirmation is unlikely to work. Indeed, the affirmation might be in absolute contradiction to what is happening in the body, *not to mention the mind!*

If affirmations do work for you, then use the affirmation, but notice if there are beliefs that contradict the affirmation. So you might be saying "I am beautiful" and a thought comes up: "But my thighs are fat." Do *Cultivating Wisdom* to dissolve that lie and notice how the affirmation feels.

If you find yourself thinking that this technique is "Too simple, it won't work, nothing ever really works", I suggest the following:

Don't get into an argument with the technique in your head as to whether it works or not, or I am right or wrong. Just do the process. Simply use the techniques and see if my statement is true or not. Test it for yourself!

Over the years I have found that many people waste time and energy arguing with strategies and claims of healing. The time spent arguing could have been much better spent **testing** the process rather than engaging in an endless dialogue, an endless story in your head with the person making the assertion.

Do I believe this or don't I believe this? Is this person right or wrong? Are they genuine or not? Is this process going to be impactful for me or not?

The point is that often we just don't know. We don't know what is going to work for us or if it is going to work for us or when it is going to work for us.

So don't believe me or dis-believe me – just try it and see what happens.

OBSTACLES

There can be obstacles to the dissolving process.

The painful feelings may be immensely overwhelming.

So you can spend a very short time in the pain and much more time in the love or power and then a very short time in the pain and more time in the love or power until you can tolerate the pain more effectively.

If none of this works, then I recommend you go and see a therapist and work one-on-one to deal with this pain in a more standard therapeutic way and then come back to this process. It will work better for you then.

The other obstacle is the mind. We have belief systems that interfere with the dissolving process.

If you get stuck with belief systems as obstacles, go back to the chapter on *Cultivating Wisdom*.

Once you have completed one example of pain, you need to go through your entire list of pain from the past and dissolve it.

You can use Power or Love to do so. There is no hard and fast rule about this as everyone is different, and although you might like or enjoy using Power now, you might want to work with Love later on.

In addition, my recommendation is that you have a core list of at least 10 items which you work with on a daily basis. The value of this is twofold. You are training yourself to dissolve pain more and more effectively and you are slowly reducing the impact of this pain from the past on your present life.

It is also very useful to notice the extent to which the pain you first experienced when recalling these memories begins to diminish over time. Seeing this change will reinforce your belief and commitment to this process.

ALTERNATIVE STRATEGY

- Feel the pain in the situation that hurts you in your life at the moment.

- Then feel the pain, linked to this present pain, *in the past.*

- Then bring in the love or power into the present situation *and* into the past, dissolving them in both places.

A DAILY EXERCISE

This is a beautiful exercise for you to do, three times a day before meals (and I'm only partly joking!).

AUDIO RECORDINGS

You can access an audio recording of this exercise. If you're reading this as an eBook, you can click on the link below to access the recording. If you are reading this on a hardcopy, type the link into your web browser to access the audio.

http://bit.ly/poemsmeditations

I welcome my sense of disempowerment that is in my being right now. I welcome the contraction, the tightness, the vulnerability, the lack of Love, the loss of Power in my being right now.

I feel my anxiety, my sense of foreboding and dread about the day. I feel my contraction about all of the negativities and threats and challenges in my life at the moment. I welcome my wanting to hide and run from all of this pain and threat.

I welcome how I want to run from life, from the realities of life. I welcome the victim that I am right now wanting to run away from life as it is.

I feel it completely in my body and in my mind. I notice and own completely the sense of anxiety, negativity, or sadness or hurt, or guilt, or shame, or emptiness, or helplessness, or vulnerability, or fragility that I feel right now.

I dissolve all **resistance** *to the negative feelings and sensations in my body right now. I simply allow them to be. (Stay with this for a few minutes before continuing. In fact, it can be very helpful to go through the above again, slowly a few times.)*

And now I begin to breathe very gently and very powerfully into in this vulnerability and disempowerment in my body. And as I breathe, so the Power or Love that I am begins to dissolve the vulnerability and lack of Power, the anxiety, the wanting to run away from life. (Pause for a while as you do this.)

And as it begins to dissolve it rises and grows and expands. It expands from my solar plexus up into my heart, into my chest and into my face and arms and legs.

I am completely infused with power at every level of my being, into the trillions of cells in my body and in my brain. My consciousness is completely infused with it. It is my consciousness.

An immense Love and Power fills my being. Like the light of the sun shining upon the world as it rises in the morning.

My entire being is awake beyond the singing of it.

I return every day more and more deeply into this energy, my true nature that I am.

CHAPTER 18

Boundaries in Action!!!

In the preface I told you the story about the greatest three minutes in my university career. I discovered what it means to understand that underneath and inside of the content of any conversation is an exchange of energy where tremendous potential for internal power and self-love lies.

And this is around creating a boundary. Not allowing others to overpower us.

What I'm going to share with you is the *how* to do it. What is really important is that these examples will work way, way better once you have learned how to access internal love and power before and during these dialogues and then in an ongoing way in your life.

My experience over many, many years, has been that the quickest and best way to learn how to do this is through examples. I will share a whole bunch of them with you now.

And please notice how, when using these techniques, I'm asking a lot of questions. I call them *Strategic Questions.*

We live in a statement culture, particularly when we are under pressure, and so we go into attack and beat people up with our aggression or we go into retreat and hide and bottle up our needs and "wants".

In essence, the questions create a more *Supportive* and softening energy. Coupled with interpreting the exchange of energy in the relationship, (saying what's going on between the two of you) they become *Challenging*.

Over decades of analysing interactions between people, I have concluded that the greatest skill in interaction with another human being is a synthesis of *Challenge* and *Support*.

Challenge is *Giving* and *Support* is *Taking*. Giving and taking make the world go around, in my opinion. People get very upset when these two qualities are not in balance.

Examples:

1. I'm in my honours year of psychology. I'm in a room specially designated for the honours students. There is coffee on tap and often chocolate cake. I love the place. It feels exclusive and I feel special. Lots of ego and a great deal of Acquired Self-Esteem.

   A PhD student in philosophy – the most intellectual of academic pursuits – is sounding off about some philosophical issue. The psychology honours students are enraptured and believing every word. They are completely disempowered.

   On that day I happened to be feeling really confident and I'm listening to this guy and I just think: "He's talking junk." I just seem to know this. I don't know why, because I can't really understand him, it's just an intuition.

   And so I say to him: "Ian, I'm really not getting what you are saying in this one particular area. Can you just explain it in simple language please?" And he looks slightly hesitant and begins to explain. And I say to him: "I'm afraid I'm still not getting it." And ask him to explain again and I do this another two or three times pushing him in the relationship

– in power – to clarify. And finally, stumbling he says: "Sorry, I have to go."

What is important here is that when I ask him to explain again in simple language, I'm not addressing any of the content of what he's saying; I'm simply not frightened of saying "I don't understand", the first point of power. Secondly, I am pushing him – my second point of power – to try harder to help us understand him.

I am working with the exchange of energy in the relationship, beneath the content.

I'm asking him to explain his *bottom line!* People tend to be extremely vague when they speak and most particularly when they're trying to manipulate you. When you push them for the bottom line, i.e. what are they really trying to say to you, you are moving them away from vagueness into clarity and in doing so you are exerting your *power*.

2. One evening our class was about to go out for dinner with a woman and her boyfriend, a top advocate at the time. He was an absolutely brilliant man who enjoyed his brilliance – who wouldn't?

Being a bunch of psychologists in one room – I call this a psych fest – the conversation naturally turned to psychology. The advocate commented that he had seen many psychologists and that he could handle any of them. He was simply expressing his superior skill in managing the psychological profession.

And out of my mouth came the comment: "Isn't it interesting that you would need to?"

He was floored, speechless. And believe me, to see an advocate speechless is a rare experience. Can you just picture the sense of power, in me, this young psychologist in training, stopping this high statured man of the legal profession in his tracks!?

It did wonders for my confidence and power and love of myself.

Most people would have gone for the content. Which would be to get into an argument about whether he actually is smarter or superior to the psychologist that he is seeing. I went for the process, the fact that he needs to *show* us and the psychologist he is seeing that he is smarter.

3. I now want to share with you one of the greatest lessons about power and boundaries and interpreting what's going on in the relationship that I have ever learned.

My girlfriend Suzie imports gas cookers from Italy. I've told you about her before. This guy, clearly very wealthy, walks into her showroom one day and very aggressively says to her: "So why is your cooker better than a Cryon cooker?" (I've just invented a new brand. Suzie doesn't like to knock the opposition.)

Later, she says to me: "I decided to make him do the work."

This is the genius. When people overpower us we are working really hard to defend our position or to attack their position or to simply run and hide, staying under the radar, in retreat.

And I say: "What do you mean?"

And here is her story.

She says: "Instead of answering his question, which would have been doing the salesperson, acrobatic, defending and explaining thing, I said, 'What car do you drive?'"

And the guy stops for a moment, which is where all of the power lies, and he looks upwards, which means he's doing the work, having to think, and he says: "A BMW!" (And of course, she guessed that he is driving a top-of-the-range car.)

And she says: "What's the difference between a BMW and a Polo?" And now he's really having to think and he's really doing all of the work and Suzie has all of the power. And he says: "Roadholding, for starters."

And she replies, while slamming the door on her super solid gas cooker, which doesn't move an inch: "Have you tried doing that with a Cryon cooker?"

The client's attitude changed completely and he was now ready for a decent dialogue about the product.

And the sale is done.

That's three questions and an "action" and the power is all in her hands. It's so simple. It's not easy, but it is simple (i.e. not complicated). We don't do it, because we are conditioned out of dialoguing like this – as I've described – because we are so addicted to responding to the content.

4. Another Suzie story. One evening she decides to have around a great chef and about eight foodie friends. The chef will cook dinner in our home and teach and explain what he's doing as he goes.

Suzie pays for the entire evening.

We have a wonderful time, with a lot of fun and food and wine – none of which I can drink because of my chronic fatigue issue – but nevertheless, it's a memorable occasion.

The evening is winding down and the chef leaves and one of the guests makes a scathingly critical comment about the food.

I turn to him and, smiling, say: "Would you like your money back?"

He is completely silenced. I have the power and I haven't insulted him or been aggressive or created an uncomfortable atmosphere in the room.

I'm indirectly illustrating the inappropriateness of his comment without directly attacking him. Most people would either do the Victim position, attack or retreat, i.e. aggression or say nothing. Can you see how much more powerful it is to do what I did?

5. My father would often attack me as a child, saying: "It's not what you say, it's how you say it." Of course, I didn't have any of these skills or any wisdom at that time, so I didn't know what to say. But just to illustrate this technique, if I had known then what I know now, I would have said to him: "And *how* you are saying this to me now is deeply disrespectful and unkind and, in fact, rather brutal and I would just love an apology."

Anytime anyone insults you, you can say this to them. Disempowered people simply feel hurt and say nothing or occasionally lash out. This is far more skilful.

6. In the following example I use what I call the *Mafia Question* to create a boundary. I used this for the first time when I returned some meditation CDs I had made. This particular company was making stickers for the CDs, with the contents of the meditation recordings on them.

There were air bubbles on the stickers.

I complained and the service provider re-did them, but the bubbles were still there. I mentioned this to him and he said that this was the best that he could do.

I said I would take the CDs elsewhere. He said that this was fine, but that I had to pay for the artwork. Out of my mouth came this spontaneous Mafia question. I said: "Are you telling me that I have to pay you for what you have done in spite of the lack of quality?" And he said, "OK" and I left smiling.

And here is a very important point. A skilful boundary is powerful *and* loving. It often leaves you smiling and without resentment. This is mastery.

The Mafia Question can sound sarcastic. Make sure that your emotions are well modulated when you use them!

The principal behind the Mafia Question is that when someone is given their "unreasonableness" back to them in the form of a summary question, there is a strong potential for them to back off from their request. So it builds personal power and negotiating capacity.

I call it the Mafia Question because I pictured the Mafia boss saying to his subordinate, Mario:

"Waste him!"

And Mario replies: "You mean I must kill him?"

It's ironic, because this is the one place the question wouldn't work. The boss would probably kill Mario!

7. The following *hypothetical question* is made by a woman in the movie *Love Actually*. She finds a necklace, a present to her husband's girlfriend. This is how she confronts him:

    "Tell me, if you were in my position, what would you do? Imagine your husband had just bought a gold necklace and he gave it to somebody else. Would you wait around to find out if it's just a necklace, or sex and a necklace and love, or would you just leave…?"

    Can you see how, in this example, she's making the other person do the work? Contrast this with the usual unskilful attack: "You bought another woman a gold necklace. You're having an affair aren't you!?"

8. One of my clients had a husband who would unilaterally make arrangements for his mother to come and spend time staying with them. She resented this endlessly and would fight with him. Creating a skilful and powerful boundary enabled her to say: "Sweetie, I wonder if I could stop you there for a moment please. Are you telling me that your mother has to stay over for the whole weekend, rather than just for one night, which I would prefer?"

This way is preferable and far more powerful than the usual kind of statement, which would be: "She can't stay for the whole weekend, that's ridiculous!"

This woman also found that when her husband expressed his guilt about not doing enough for his mother, she would try to rescue him. The Self-Esteem work helped her to stop doing the rescue thing. Some months after we did this work, she said to me that when she stopped rescuing him, he got tougher with his mother and felt less guilt.

And here's the kicker. She said: "Stopping rescuing him helped him more than when I was desperately trying to make him feel better!"

Rescuing *disables* others.

9. Have you ever noticed how often people refuse to answer your questions? To let them get away with this is to give away your power to them. I remember watching a nego-tiation in a business situation where the salesperson was trying to close a deal, and whenever he asked the client if he was ready to go ahead, the client would wander off into all sorts of related and unrelated topics.

The salesperson finally said, with a smile on his face: "I'm not sure if that's a yes, you want to go ahead, or no you don't?" He closed the deal instantly.

People also often hear something that doesn't make sense and say *nothing* because they fear looking stupid.

10. There are occasions when it is extremely skilful and very powerful to dig deeper into the content.

A while back I heard a journalist on the radio interviewing an expert on the mining industry regarding the nationalising of a mine. The interviewee said at one point "The mine was **showing promise for a while**", to which the interviewer replied: "And why did the re-structuring take 10 years?"

The interviewer missed the bottom line. A much better set of questions would have been:

"Was the mine showing promise before or after it was nationalised? How long before or after it was nationalised was it doing well? How badly did it do? You don't think that there were perhaps other factors that led to the mine not doing well?"

It absolutely boggles me how often I see really bright people miss asking these kinds of questions. It's extraordinary. And I think the reason is that they are hi-jacked by their emotional response to what is being said and they miss the big picture and so much of the time people are in retreat, fearing being offensive – remember *The Girl with the Dragon Tattoo* movie.

11. I had another wonderful moment of learning with Professor Straker, whom I mentioned in my story in the preface of this book. I had a client, again in my fifth year, who was

a student at the university who had a lot of emotional problems, including that of significant aggression.

It was suggested by the professor that I send her to the hospital for an EEG, because we had suspicions that she might be suffering from temporal lobe epilepsy, which often has aggressive outbursts associated with it. She didn't want to do this, but I managed to convince her to do so. She went for the EEG and walked into my office for the next session in a rage.

She grabbed the whiteboard eraser in her right hand and looked as though she was about to throw it at me and started shouting at me: "Why didn't you tell me that they would stick all of these electrodes on my head? It was the most terrible experience, I hate you!"

In my young, unskilful and inexperienced anxiety I started to apologise to her, which simply raised her level of aggression, while I continued to apologise.

Professor Straker stopped the video recorder and said to me: "Mark, how many times have you apologised to her?"

To which I replied rather anxiously and hesitantly: "I don't know – about six or seven times?"

And she said: "Precisely. Two apologies would have been enough and then what you should have said to her was: 'I've apologised twice. I wonder what else you are wanting from me?'"

Utter genius!

What I realised is that I had spent much of my life, when threatened or too eager to please others, doing the rescuer position on the victim triangle, and this was the start of my transformation. Dr Demartini has coined the most beautiful word for this: self-wrongeousness, which is simply the opposite of self-righteousness.

Notice the question. She's not saying what many people might have said *accusatorily*: "I've apologised to you enough. This is your problem!"

The question puts the monkey on the other person's back in a *respectful* yet *powerful* way and, as described earlier, "You are making them do the work!"

12. When people are trying to bully and manipulate and manoeuvre you, the best thing to do is to tell them what they are doing. So here is an example from one of my clients.

This woman's boyfriend had been selfish and narcissistic in multiple ways. The final straw came when the night before her 11-year-old son Kyle's birthday, the boyfriend cancelled, saying that he had to go to a boxing match rather than attend the birthday party.

Here is her comment:

"Can you see that your not attending the birthday party is deeply distressing to Kyle and it reflects how much of the time you put yourself first in our relationship and that coming second is, for me, unacceptable?"

This has to be said with an even and modulated tone, which is why getting the *energetic signature* of love and internal power *right,* is so important. If it is said sarcastically or angrily, it's just the victim position of attack.

13. Have you ever had people not respond to your emails and text messages, over and over and over again? Here's what I do to elicit a response from them. It works 90% of the time.

"Hi Dave. It would be really, really awesome if you could respond to my text messages! (or emails, if that is the medium you've been using)."

You notice how I am not attacking Dave and I'm not repeating what I am asking for and I'm not attacking him by saying that he is ignoring me. I'm going for the exchange of energy in the relationship, which is an implied statement *about* his ignoring me.

14. Managing people's performance is one of the most difficult things you can ever encounter in a business. Mostly, managers go into avoidance around doing this and simply complain to others or internally in their heads about the lack of performance.

I worked with a manager named Sarah who was deeply frustrated by her subordinate and tried everything she knew to try to improve this woman's performance. Nothing worked. Finally, she approached the subordinate and said to her:

"You know, we've had so many conversations around your performance and we really haven't gone anywhere and I'm sure you are as stressed about it as I am, yes? What I would love to do is something I don't think I've done very well, which is to really try to understand the stresses and difficulties you're having in this job. So can I book a conference room up the road for a few hours this week so that I can really try to understand you better?"

Notice how much support there is in this interaction, owning the ways she is responsible for the problem: "...something I haven't done very well..."

The subordinate agreed and off they went a few days later. Sarah spent the first *hour and a half* simply asking questions around her subordinate's stress and struggles both on and off the job, and when she could feel that the trust had been rebuilt through her *supportive* and kind and warm listening and understanding, she then moved into *challenging* the subordinate by saying:

"As I understand it, what you're needing from me and from the business is the following (and she then described and summarised everything that the subordinate had been asking for) and I will do my best to deliver this.

Can I now tell you what I am needing differently from you in order for us to move forward in a completely different way?"

Can you see what she is doing? These are the two key components of really skilful communication. It's the ability to *Support* and when the trust has been built to then *Challenge*.

This particular subordinate transformed and eventually, when the manager got promoted, took over her position.

Support skilfully … and then when there is trust, Challenge.

15. I had a client, a woman aged 45, who was trying to start a new career as a coach. Her husband was bringing up all of the negatives and pitfalls and potential failures. Finally, one day she said to him: "You've expressed a lot of doubt about me making a success of this work. Are you absolutely sure that I'm not going to make a success of it?" And he replied, slowly: "I'm not too sure."

And she said: "Then I'm wondering why you can't see that obviously I'm thinking of the potential problems, but in your raising them endlessly I feel unsupported and, more than anything, I would love your support in this thing that is really scaring me."

And he softened and apologised.

Doing this work in an intimate relationship is much more difficult than outside of one because the emotions run much deeper and often a partner is not going to respond as we wish.

Sometimes people come into our lives not for us to succeed in our communications with them but for us to build our skill to deal with the rest of life!

In addition, you need to check what "success" means. In other words, success with the really difficult bully might simply mean that you stop them from bullying you or that you choose to leave the relationship but feel that you have loved yourself and lived from internal power.

I believe that it is really important to give people, including bullies, the freedom to behave any way they want to, and then I have the freedom to behave any way I want to, in response to them, including walking out of the relationship, with a smile on my face – now that's love and power!

16. I want to take you back to a story from the time when I was living in the Rhenosterspruit Nature Reserve.

I was on this committee trying to build the nature reserve into a cohesive and functional unit. Quite a challenge, I must tell you.

So it's one Sunday and a few of the members of the committee and an outsider consultant guy named Gerrit were visiting for lunch. And we got to talking about nature reserve matters and Gerrit says to me in a very direct and kind way: "Mark, you don't speak up enough in the meetings."

And I get all defensive and I say: "Yeah, but I can't understand all of this technical stuff about fencing materials and costs and bulldozers and labour supply, etc."

And Gerrit, to his credit, doesn't stop there and says: "You can always speak what's in your heart."

And I think to myself, wow, he's right!

You see, this committee was filled with a bunch of cowboys – whom I was really intimidated by – and who wanted to go and spend a few hundred thousand rands on building a game fence around the entire reserve, and my intuition told me that it was premature, but I didn't open my mouth and I could have.

I could have simply spoken to the process and said: "You know people, I think it's too soon. I just have the feeling that we shouldn't rush into this and spend all of this money when it could become a disaster because we haven't planned it carefully enough."

And guess what? We put up 3 km of fencing and 2 km would get stolen and would put up another 2 km another 1 km would get stolen, and why? Because we hadn't taken the time to get the buy-in of all the local labourers and community so that they would support and understand what the project was about.

Within six months the entire fence had been built and slowly dismantled!

Not speaking my intuition was disempowered and what a lesson I learned from dear Gerrit, who I heard was shot in a car-jacking incident a couple of years later. Bless him.

The authentic expression of what is in your heart
is a gift to the world.

The best way to learn how to do this work is to practise. Start asking *Strategic Questions* and make skilful statements and don't get hooked into arguing the content, but also dismantle people's nonsense with innocent, probing questions.

17. I'm facilitating a conflict between two business partners. The first one, whom I'll call George, starts off the process with a long story about responsibilities in the business and who's doing what and how much time he is spending on admin issues and not building the business. It's long and convoluted and difficult to follow.

The second partner, Stan, with whom I've been doing some coaching work, says: "Are you saying you are unhappy about the inequitable workload between us?"

George agrees and they begin to dialogue strategies for relieving him of his admin workload.

Stan is using a *Summarising Question*, to make George feel understood, to get clarity for himself and to bring the confusion in the discussion, into a place of clarity.

This is a brilliant strategy to use any time you are confused, or don't understand someone, or simply want to build trust in the relationship.

18. Many years ago I had a major conflict with a business partner – I'll call him Derek. He attacked me in a meeting, seemingly out of the blue and then walked out. He avoided me for the next three weeks. I knew we had to sort it out so I called a meeting with him and the first thing I said was:

"Would you mind if I started the discussion?"

"Sure thing," he said. Not looking certain at all.

"I just wanted to say that I would like to apologise to you for putting you under pressure about the big deal." (He was trying to close a very big deal, which all of us had been waiting for. It was going to make us all very rich.)

"I really didn't like the way you spoke to me in our last meeting, but I do believe I put you under undue pressure to make the deal happen and I really do want to apologise for that."

He looked stunned and replied: "Wow, thank you. I really appreciate that and I don't know what would've happened if you hadn't said that, but I want to apologise too because, you know, since I've been back from my holiday I know I've been taking people out at the knees."

What is so important in this issue is that I felt he was 95% responsible for attacking me, but I started with the 5% for which I was responsible. (It is important to add that he had on many occasions reassured us that we could rely on him to do the deal.)

I have found this to be an extraordinarily powerful way in which to deal with conflict and to calm people down. Just make a sincere apology about your "stuff", no matter how small it is. It is more probable that they will then own their issues as well.

CHAPTER 19

Scenarios from Your Early Years

It is really very useful to dissolve the pain and the anxiety and helplessness around scenarios from our childhood. Go back to the following situations (and particularly each room in your home) and in your life and check out the extent to which you experienced any of the above feelings as well as trauma, grief, abandonment, betrayal, shame and guilt, from your family/ home situation.

Notice the energetic signature in your family home or wherever you were brought up.

Notice the feelings and messages and rigidity and forms of control exerted upon you and find your disempowerment there and dissolve yourself back into Power. Dissolve as much of your pain in each room of your home(s) as you can, so that you can imagine moving around your entire home just feeling more Power and Love.

MEAL TIMES – the kitchenette or the dining room

This is an incredibly important space for most people. Great pain is often experienced around meal times.

Take yourself in your memory back into this space. Notice how much tension, anxiety, aggression there was in your parents/

caregivers/siblings/yourself. Were you frightened of getting into trouble?

Did you live in fear around mealtimes, of being lectured to, threatened?

How fearful were you of your parents/caregivers, of conflict and tension between them!

Notice the degree to which you took on their pain, tension, stress.

Dissolve as much of this in power and love so that you shine like the sun, retrospectively in that situation.

Can you reach the point where you can visualise yourself saying in that situation:

> *"I am a powerhouse, filled with love for no reason, as I eat my meals as a child!"*

YOUR BEDROOM

Notice the pain you experienced in your bedroom, the isolation or the overcrowding, the sense of feeling abandoned or the sense that this was the only private space in which you could be with your pain.

Often this can be a very private, special place, but it can contain a sense of rigid withdrawal, an aloneness which can lead to depression and fear of engaging the world.

Feel the pain here and dissolve it as best you can in power and love.

Can you reach the point where you visualise yourself saying:

*"I love my bedroom. I love myself in my bedroom.
I am power in my bedroom."*

And if this applies...

*"My bedroom is no longer a place to hide; it is a place
of healing and love, from which I venture
with confidence into the world."*

THE SITTING ROOM OR THE FAMILY ROOM

Notice any issues around this place in your home.

What were the feelings around watching TV?

What pain was contained in issues around programmes on television?

Did they create nightmares? If so, dissolve the pain of those nightmares.

Was the conflict in the family around which programmes could be watched by whom and when?

If so, dissolve the pain around this conflict.

Was there a sense of isolation or great conflict or both in this space?

Feel the pain here and dissolve it as best you can in power or love.

"I am a powerhouse in the sitting room. I love this place."

ILLNESS

Notice how disempowered you felt when you or someone else was ill.

Notice the energetic signature in the family around illness.

Perhaps it was the only time you felt cared for and loved.

Did that make you "want" to be sick more often?

Did you feel abandoned being sick?

Heal and dissolve the abandonment in love and *be* the love.

Notice the emotional pain you experienced in your reaction to the physical pain.

Did illness isolate you or bring you love? Did it depress you? Dissolve it all.

> *"I feel all illness I experienced as a child - and in the present - dissolving it in love and power."*

SCHOOL, SPORT, FRIENDS

Go into the classrooms, the playground and the sports field.

Notice which you feared the most, the teachers you feared the most, the headmaster's/mistress's office?

Notice the fear of failure, the panic around wanting to succeed and the desire for success.

Notice the terror of performance anxiety!!!

Notice your sense of connection and disconnection to friends. Your sense of being approved of and rejected by your peers.

Feel the pain of judgment, of failure, of being beaten, ostracised, bullied.

Feel the longing for romantic love, the fantasies associated with this. Dissolve the fantasies.

Dissolve the negative feelings.

Notice how you approved of or judged yourself. Notice the guilt and shame.

Dissolve as much of it as you can until you *know that you are love.*

"I dissolve all of the pain I ever felt as a student at school."

SEXUALITY

Our society is one big, major panic attack around sexuality.

It is feared, hidden, lied about, covered up, fantasised about, repressed, suppressed, denied, projected … it is endless.

The energetic signature is contorted, twisted, guilty, shamed, desperate, longing, confused, ecstatic and chaotic.

Feel the messages that you received about sex and sexuality.

As a young girl, if your dress was just one inch too short, there might have been messages of slut, whore, cheap, easy … did you receive any of these messages? If so, dissolve the pain and the judgement and the beliefs around this.

Did you get raped or feel violated in any way. Dissolve the pain.

As a guy, did you feel "manly" enough or virile, or desirable enough? If you were raped as a boy or man, (one out of every 10 victims of rape are men) notice the guilt, the shame, the sense of not being a man that this evoked.

If there was any sexual abuse, notice any pleasure you derived from it and dissolve any guilt you experienced as a result of this pleasure.

We think that because abuse is "bad", it should not in any way have been pleasurable.

Dissolve the garbage, the lies you have been fed about sex, the pain and the rejection of yourself in love and power. Dissolve your pain and the pain of unrealised fantasies in love and power and joy.

> "I love my sexuality. I dissolve all of my judgements about my sexual oddities and perversions and the ways in which I broke the rules, in love and power."

RELIGION AND SPIRITUALITY

Was religion forced on you?

If so, was it painful?

Did you feel controlled, violated, disrespected in this process?

Go back to places of worship and heal any of the pain *and the unrequited longing* there.

Our longing for salvation and the failure of these prayers can be immensely and immeasurably painful to us.

Dissolve the pain of the longing and dissolve any other pain around these issues.

Note: I spent many years immersed in the pain and longing for spiritual enlightenment. I felt that the suffering this involved was noble.

It was not.

It gave me nothing.

What changed this was the discovery of Adyashanti's meditative and spiritual teachings. So if you're filled with longing for God or Awakening, I suggest that you use the meditation technique that I've been working with here and notice that when you do "Just sitting", a Presence or Stillness arises, which is God, which is Soul.

When we are locked into our longing, it is the ego longing for the connection to God and...

It isn't the ego that connects with God.

We experience the connection with Soul or God when the ego gets out of the way!

That's my experience.

MANNERS AND GOOD BEHAVIOUR

Are you a good boy or a good girl?

Manners that are trained into us at an early age can cause the most intense contractions in the body/mind.

The body creates an armour of pretence, a fake image that is now presented to the world. You might know or discover that my email address is realmark@icon.co.za.

Why such a strange address?

Because when I created it, I was really focussed on dumping the 'Fake-Mark' part of me, ingrained into my psyche by my parents.

What is a sensitive little boy going to do in response to the judgements of his parents?

As he was told.

Becoming good and kind and well, fake!

If this applies to you, notice how it feels in your body. Notice the body armour that develops. Dissolve the armour in love and power. Dissolve your fears around being honest, authentic, open and real that contradict being a good boy or girl.

Heal the pain of your over-respectful way of being in the world and watch to see if you become looser and more spontaneous.

Decades ago, when I first went into my own psychotherapy, I started to deal with this pain. I went to lunch one Sunday to a friend.

The next day I had to collect something from her.

I told her that I had had a good time at the party. She said it was a pleasure and then she mentioned a couple that I had been talking to and said they had liked me but said I was a bit "rude".

I celebrated this feedback.

Why?

Because I had grown up such a good little boy, so well tailored and mannered and well presented, that being seen as rude was in my opinion a compliment!

I was learning to be more real, less protected and armoured against criticism and so there was now a risk of being perceived as rude.

INTELLECT AND SCHOOL PERFORMANCE

Notice the energy in your home around this issue. How much do you value your intellect? I know PhDs who think they aren't smart enough, always needing to show off how clever they are – one of the hallmarks of Acquired Self-Esteem. Feel the pain here and dissolve it in power and love as best you can and keep working at it. This "working at it" applies to all of the work in this book.

There is so much "quick-fix" – seven secrets to solving your relationships issues – type of stuff out there. My experience says that it takes time.

FOOD AND BODY SHAPE AND BEAUTY

Were you given messages that you were ugly, fat, thin, short, clumsy, scrawny, nerdy?

A business partner of my second ex-wife once said to her that I was a nerd. I resented it and felt hurt. Now ... I love the idea!

If you picture yourself eating dessert, or a second helping of food, or eating sweets, or refusing to eat, what was the energetic signature from your mother or father or both of them around these issues?

Were/are you bulimic, anorexic? If so, what's the energetic signature around this and can you dissolve all of the need to use food to control relationships around you?

Dissolve all of the pain around food, so that you are just left with the joy of nourishing yourself through food.

Many people are fixated on deriving pleasure from food, because they don't get it elsewhere in their lives.

Is this you?

If so, can you dissolve the pain of longing for pleasure from food? Can you feel the pleasure you get from food, without it being a desperate process?

Can you be joy, without needing more and more ... endless pleasure?

This is a tricky process. If you have health issues, then your body is going to be craving sugars and fats and salt. So this can be physiological *and* psychological and you might really need to focus on healing your physical issues in order to be able to more skilfully work with the psychological.

Some people have major issues about being very beautiful or good looking. Their egos are oversized because of all of the appreciation they get for how they look. When we are over-appreciated we can get manic, which can lead to deflation and depression thereafter.

So what you might want to do is dissolve all of the excessive pleasure you get from how good you look and how much approval and appreciation you get and return back to the central position that is neither manic nor depressed but is simply love for yourself as you are.

INTIMATE RELATIONSHIPS

Go through every painful one. Write them down. Parents, teachers, lovers, friends, business associates, children. (Children seldom give us exactly what we want from them.)

Heal the pain from each one. Go back to your divorce(s). Heal the pain from each one.

People get divorced and then re-marry really fast. The pain and the hurt from the first marriage is unresolved. The second marriage is a desperate attempt to escape this pain.

It seldom works.

Some people never remarry. They nurture their wounds from the divorce, as their new partner.

They never let go.

If this is you, can you dissolve this pain ... now?

ILLNESSES/OPERATIONS

Heal the pain from each one. Go through each one and heal any residual hurt and pain physical, mental, emotional.

Operations are traumatic.

You may need to consult a trauma specialist to work with this.

CHAPTER 20

Cultivating Wisdom

Here's a summary of the key aspects of the *Cultivating Wisdom* technique.

- Take a belief that you got from your parents, caregiver, teachers, books, spiritual texts, or that you created for yourself, that causes you guilt or anxiety or pain.

- See if you can find who it came from.

- Ask yourself why they were telling you this. Was it for you or for them? It was most probably for them and not for you and so see the selfishness and the pain in the injunction.

- Even if it didn't come from someone else, do the following: Feel the lie in your body. Spend some time feeling that this is a lie and dissolve it and give it back to the person who gave it to you or if you created it yourself, then simply dissolve it.

Can you feel the lie that says: "You have to have a reason to love yourself!?"

- It is often useful to do a dialogue with them as you might have it now in returning that belief system to them.

- Notice every time you feel guilty or anxious about doing or not doing something, saying or not saying something, and check what the belief is behind that guilt.

- Dissolve the belief in love and power and discover what *your truth* is.

And then feel the love and power of living YOUR unique truth!

You may need to practise this many times. Why? Because you have embedded this into your psyche and body *hundreds and thousands of times!*

It takes time to undo your bad "eating habits". Why eating habits? Because we swallow food after chewing it, and we also swallow ideas and beliefs. Mostly, we don't chew or taste them, we just swallow them whole, or reject them completely.

If you were to bite on a piece of fish and it tasted off, you would spit it out. But these insane ideas that come from our parents and from our culture, we just swallow them whole – and they are rotten!!!

We ignore the taste of them, we ignore whether they feel nourishing and good and right for us, *because we live in fear and we long for approval and acceptance more than we resent the indigestion and pain and poison that we get infected with* because we are just kids and we have little power and little wisdom.

- So with this technique you are going back and checking, how does it feel to ingest this lie, and you spit out the lie and own your power and independence, and every time the belief and the pain comes up, you spit out the poisonous lie as you own your power and learn what you want to ingest from the outside and what you want to chew on.

- One of my biggest lessons as a management consultant was that I noticed the differences between managers and subordinates. I watched many teams and their managers. When there was threat or pressure – it was usually only the manager who had strong, creative opinions – the subordinates were passive; they lived in fear and said nothing.

If you asked them how they felt in the meeting, they would have had no awareness of any fear or of being controlled by their conditioning. They would say:

"My manager is dictatorial" or "an idiot" or "authoritarian" or "She's the smart one", all of which might be true, but the problem was primarily in them!

They had ingested the beliefs of: "Don't be honest with someone in authority, or don't challenge someone older than you. Be afraid to make mistakes. Don't make career-limiting moves."

SUMMARY

There's this lovely joke: How many psychologists does it take to change a light bulb?

Just one, but the bulb really has to want to change!

That really sums up the key differentiator for transformation.

How much do you want it? In working with thousands of people over the years I have discovered that we bring an attitude to this work that infiltrates everything that happens while we're doing it.

When I start to use this *Cultivating Wisdom* process with some people, they really don't want to listen to me. They really are addicted to their belief systems and to being rigidly embedded in them.

So as I start to help them to dismantle their beliefs, you can see and feel a tremendous energy around staying as they are and a lack of openness and fluidness around the possibility of change.

So you might want to ask yourself, honestly, how much do I want to dissolve the beliefs that I have that are not useful, that are not functional? Unfortunately, beliefs are an addiction and, as I'm sure you know, one of the primary components of addiction is denial.

Ask yourself the following questions if you struggle to dissolve your belief systems that are obstacles to transformation:

- Is this belief a part of my identity and if so, what anxieties would I need to dissolve in order to let go of the belief?

- What would it mean to dissolve this belief?

- What changes would I have to make in my life if I dissolved this belief?

- Would I judge myself for having lived with an erroneous belief for such a long time if I gave up this particular belief?

- *Go back to being a child when you ingested the belief and notice the disempowerment there. Bring power into yourself at that age and then dissolve the belief in the past and in the present.*

- And when you've done some of this work and you're making some progress, say:

> *I see all of the beliefs that have been conditioned into me. Every belief that is not in alignment with my truth is now dissolved back into this truth.*

CHAPTER 21

Reclaiming Your Power

AUDIO RECORDING

You can access an audio recording of this meditation. If you're reading this as an eBook, you can click on the link below to access the recording. If you are reading this on a hardcopy, type the link into your web browser to access the audio.

http://bit.ly/poemsmeditations

I remember as far back as I can in my life, the first times that I gave away my self-worth, my power and my value when I felt uncertain and judged and criticised and rejected. I remember the feeling of not being appreciated, of not being approved of, and surrendering all that was beautiful in me to others and to the world.

I notice how the energetic signature of doubt and disbelief in myself began to emerge in me as I learned to give away my Power and self-worth. I remember how it appeased others and they would then be kind to me and more loving when I subordinated myself to them. And I remember how I enjoyed the appreciation and affection I received as I did this.

So as I gave away my self-worth and I received something in return, some measure of affection, some sense of being okay and approved of. But I also remember how temporary it was and I notice the addiction to having to be appreciated and loved and, most importantly, that in manipulating others to get this love, I was giving away my sense of value and worth.

I notice how the giving away of my value and worth was far greater than what I received, yet I was powerless to do anything about it. I forgive myself, I honour myself, I love myself for all of the thousands of times I have given away my self-worth to others.

I see this giving away that I did as a child, as I grew up as an adolescent. I gave it away to my parents, to my teachers, to my peers, to strangers. I gave it away to the written word, which I believed, because it was written down on paper, in a book, by someone, was a so-called "authority".

I notice the thousands of times I have given away my power and self-worth to someone whom I thought was more impor-tant than me, more special than me, more worthwhile than me, more valid than me.

I notice the thousands of times I have given away my vali-dation. The sense of knowing that I exist and am valid as a human being.

I notice the thousands of times and feel and remember the energetic signature of the thousands of times I felt invalid in the face of someone else's supposed validity.

I remember and notice how I gave away my self-worth and power and love of myself as I went into the world of work and responsibility. How I needed and wanted to prove that I was okay and was fearful that I wasn't, and in this needing and wanting, the self-worth was gone and I contracted into a ball of agony and pain as I longed and hoped for the affirmation from others.

I remember and notice the energetic signature of craving success and fearing failure. And I notice that every time I did this, every time I've thought about the consequences of my actions, I gave away the simple Joy of just being, without any thought for consequence or success.

I notice how I have thousands and thousands of times taken on the sense, from the rest of the world, that everything I do must be scored and rated and judged. I have scored myself out of 10, scored myself as a percentage, scored myself as a winner or loser or as a success or a failure.

And now I very slowly, very, very slowly begin to reclaim my power and discover that I am love and power. There is an energetic signature to reclaiming the sense of worth and I begin to feel what it is like to reclaim the hundreds of thousands of times I have given away my sense of value. It is like a vast, immense river of power returning to its source, which is the light inside of me, and the light is beginning to grow and live and shine with the quality and strength and energy that is beyond the imagining of it, beyond the measuring of it. It is simply a resurgence of the Original Truth that I am.

I am discovering that my job is to love myself for no reason. If I need a good reason, a logical reason to love myself, I am lost. Why? Because if I have to look to reason, to logic, to the mind, to love myself, then logic will soon find a reason to say that I am not loveable, not worthy.

So I notice what it feels like to love myself, to shine like the sun, for no reason whatsoever. This love is simply who I am.

I completely release the need to rate and score and compare myself to others. This is freedom, to be whatever I am, whatever happens.

The power flows back into me from all of those times given away, it fills my being. I am resurrected. I am returned to the

Truth. I shine and radiate and resonate in this magnificent reclaiming of all of the power given away by me to situations and people and events.

And now I rest gently in this power and love for who I am, for what I am, for the truth of my nature. I shine with the reclaiming. I am filled to the brim with this reclaiming. I am overflowing with power and with this light.

If you enjoyed this meditation, if you really felt the energy of it, then don't...

just...

do...

it...

once!!!

As you move away from this meditative journey, you want to notice the tendency, a habit that is deeply formed inside of you, that makes you want to give away the power again and again and again. Perhaps you are checking your emails and some anxiety emerges as you do this or you are relating to your partner or a subordinate or manager in a way that suggests that they are more worthy than you, and in that moment you give away your power.

So what you want to be able to do, in an ongoing way, is to begin to reclaim the power as you notice yourself giving it away, because you have done it so many times before, over and over and over again.

CHAPTER 22

If Only this One Thing Would Change ... I Would be Happy!

POWER AND LOVE – WITHOUT CAUSE

This technique was the start, the origin of this entire process.

- Find one thing in your life that you are wanting right now and believing that if you could get this thing or fix this problem, you would be happy. A health issue, a money issue, a career issue, just to finish this one, long, difficult project...

- Feel the wanting, this desperate wanting, as deeply as you can.

- Just feeling the wanting and allow it to dissolve spontaneously.

Feel the energy of it being "sorted"
without it having to be "sorted".

OR

- Go back and forth between "wanting" and "having" and then just stay with the "having".

> *When we release desperate wanting, we make space*
> *for inspired wanting to happen.*

> *Rest as the love and power that you are before anything has*
> *happened on the outside.*

- On an ongoing basis, just notice your fantasy that "If I could fix this one thing..." and dissolve your fantasy in power. Fantasies are disempowered. A fantasy is the opposite of power.

> *Dissolving fantasies is one of the most*
> *power-inducing things you can do.*

CHAPTER 23

Projecting Self-Esteem

Write down the names of people, situations and *positive* character traits that you wish you had, that others have: beauty, popularity, power, good times, focus, energy, money, IQ, success ... and names of famous people. Super models, Einstein, Mandela, Mother Theresa, Branson, Ghandi...

Take one of those people or one of the traits and feel the envy and wanting to reach outside of yourself for what they have and notice how you are creating a sense of worthlessness when you do that.

And then upload the beauty or genius in yourself. If you can't do that, download it from them, get the energy from them and then upload into yourself.

If you're still struggling to do it, remember a time when you had that quality. This can take a bit of work, but it is very powerful. And the reason it takes work is that the projection is very powerful. In the same way as we struggle to see our own selfishness to the degree that we see it in other people, we also tend to struggle to see and feel our own beauty and success and power that we have projected onto other people.

Every time you go to Facebook and you feel the envy, just upload that energy that you are projecting ... into yourself.

You might not have the beauty or power in the form that the other person has it, but there is no question that you have it in other forms. Because the mind tends to see what's missing, but if you look you will find it.

I was working with a client who had just resigned as a CEO from his job.

He was very deflated about his ability and his struggles in the business he'd been in and talked to me about the fact that he felt like a complete failure.

Because the mind always looks for what's missing, all he could see was the sense of failure in this previous job. I knew that success was there; he just wasn't seeing it, and I said to him "Okay, let's find the success", and he looked at me very doubtfully. Nevertheless, we proceeded.

We managed to find six areas in which he was very successful. He said he was incredibly good with numbers and strategic thinking and supply chain management and at going to the gym five days a week and building his strength and physical appearance and at caring for his family. This softened his sense of failure.

Own your projections and stop giving away your self-worth.

OWNING INNOCENCE

I would like to conclude with an amazing story and a truly wonderful quality to own in yourself – *innocence*.

I was working with a woman who was struggling with the loss of her dog named Pookie. She had an amazing intuitive connection with this animal. She was in enormous pain and loss at the animal's passing. So I asked her to find the qualities in all of the animals she had ever known that she admired most and felt were missing in herself.

She came up with love, acceptance and playfulness, and so I asked her to feel these qualities in the animal that had passed away and then to find those qualities in herself and to allow them to expand and grow inside of her. This she did very beautifully.

I then asked her if she had not felt the incredible quality of innocence in Pookie. She said yes, she had done this. I then asked her to feel that quality of innocence inside of herself, to find it in herself. This she was able to do (if you struggle to do this, then simply find any moment in your life when you felt you were innocent, perhaps when you were a child or when you had a sense that your mind was not busy asking questions and you were simply feeling curious about something beautiful in the world).

I asked her to expand this quality of innocence inside of her. And also to feel the incredible, spacious Stillness in the innocence and to notice as this feeling expanded and how it is completely the antithesis of what the mind does. Innocence is without any conceptual process happening. It is without rumination, without any mental movement. And what's most important, it's just so powerful.

I asked her to resonate in the energy of this spacious, magnificent, mindless experience and then to feel the connection with Pookie's innocence. Her innocence connecting with his innocence.

This is oneness, wholeness.

This is our true spiritual home that we long for. She did this beautifully and the transformation in her experience was amazing.

It was extraordinarily moving for me and for her. And her grief softened as she went through this process.

What I realised is when we look at our dogs or cats or the horses we own, and we hold them and hug them and cling to them and want to devour them, we do so because we have disowned the innocence in ourselves. Wwe then project it onto them and then try to get it back from them. Trying to get it back is the clinging, contracting toward the innocence in them and the innocence we have projected into them.

I do think that in clinging to this innocence in our animals we are also running from the world of people, filled with control and conflict and rejection and criticism, which is so painful to us.

When I started to do this with my three cats, Amy, Guinevere and Frank, my relationship with them changed. It became less needy, more equal and more of a connection of innocence to innocence.

As I became more whole, my connection with them became more whole. There was previously this division between me and them because I thought that they had qualities that I didn't have, but which I was projecting onto them. We now share and connect with each other from the innocence we all have.

I now know that when they die, I will be able to feel the energy that we share that is between us and in all of us, and I have no doubt that pain of loss will be reduced because of it and perhaps it will dissolve completely.

To a large degree, grief can be softened by owning the qualities you think are missing in your life when in fact they are inside of you and indeed, as I learned from Dr Demartini, somewhere in your life in another form.

I had another client, a businessman of about 40, an engineer, very focused on his intellect and on logic. These qualities drove his life and created much of his pain.

We started to work with the quality of innocence, and it was fascinating to watch him use it in many arenas of his life. When he found himself ruminating anxiously about whether his girl-friend was about to reject him or not, he simply connected with the innocence in himself and dissolved his paranoia this way.

I've also had clients use innocence to help them to fall asleep. Why? Because when we are ruminating endlessly as we lie awake at night, the mind is very busy and there is not an iota of innocence to be found.

Innocence is spacious and Still and doesn't ruminate about anything. Just look at your cat or your dog sitting quietly just looking out of the window or looking at nothing in particular. There appears to be no "mind chatter", just being in the present moment, infinitely spacious and at peace.

TECHNIQUE FOR OWNING INNOCENCE

- Sit down with your favourite dog or cat or horse or just sit with a child below the age of one year. If you can't be with them, imagine doing it.

- Cuddle them the way you normally do. Notice your wanting to consume or devour the innocent goodness in them.

- Dissolve this need in love or power and then just feel the innocence in them and see if you can find that same energy inside of you. If you can't do it, then a few minutes of meditation will help and you will find it easier. Innocence is part of our nature and it's there. If you can't feel it, it's just buried beneath years of anxiety and pain and a billion overwhelming thoughts.

- Now just feel the innocence in you connecting to the innocence in the animal or to the infant.

- Use it in the following ways:

  - To dissolve your judgements of yourself. Innocence is entirely non-judgemental because it's not thinking. To judge, you have to think.

  - To dissolve your judgements of others.

- To slow down your mind when it's all just too much for you up there – particularly if you're trying to fall asleep.

- To soften your need to analyse everyone else and yourself and life and to get lost in the stories you tell yourself about life.

CHAPTER 24

From Pain to Love & Power 2.0

This work is about dissolving pain in the present.

- Write down the feelings and issues you are struggling with in your life right now. For example, you feel inferior, powerless, helpless, lonely, shamed, judgemental, isolated, being a pushover, stressed, anxious, overloaded, breaking down … life is dangerous, you fear exposure, embarrassment, you rescue others, you don't deserve goodness or success, you don't finish things … or you want more excitement, you want to leave a legacy but feel that you are failing, you don't feel special enough or you don't have a significant enough life, you have many fantasies that are unfulfilled and so you are disappointed, deflated or depressed.

- Dissolve each of these issues in your baseline feelings of power or love and use *Cultivating Wisdom* questions to dissolve belief-system obstacles to whatever is left over.

- In addition, if you feel powerless, look for the areas in your life where you feel powerful. Remember that we tend to notice what's missing. Find the areas in your life where you feel the opposite of this pain.

- Write down the traits you hate about yourself. Selfish, cruel, manipulative, distant etc, and dissolve your judgements in love.

CHAPTER 25

I Only Exist if You Approve of Me: Meditative Process

AUDIO RECORDING

You can access an audio recording of this meditation. If you're reading this as an eBook, you can click on the link below to access the recording. If you are reading this on a hardcopy, type the link into your web browser to access the audio.

http://bit.ly/poemsmeditations

Can you go back to your first memory of disapproval? Picture the first person who judged you, rejected you, who "Raped your Self-Esteem". Can you feel, in the sense of disapproval, how it feels to not exist in their eyes?

Feel the sense of needing and wanting them to love you and hating the pain of their rejection of you. Feel the longing for them to love you or simply to be nice to you. This longing is understandable, but a terrible mistake. Because now you are chained to your longing for approval and essentially you are saying I don't exist until I get the sense of approval from the other person.

So can you feel this pain, this feeling of rejection in this longing and can you begin to dissolve it in power or love or innocence?

Can you feel that it is a sandwich-board thought that some-one must approve of you in order for you to exist? If it's a sandwich-board thought, it is not the truth. You have lived a lie for so much of your life. As you see the truth, can you feel the dissolution of the belief that you can only exist if you are approved of?

"The truth shall set you free." Can you see and feel and know how true that is? As you see the lie that you have lived, so the truth emerges and frees you from the bondage of the lies that you have lived all of your life.

And now can you picture a school teacher who rejected you, whom you longed to love you and appreciate you or just ac-cept you? Can you feel the sense of not existing in the face of who they were and picture yourself sitting at that school desk feeling desperate and miserable and in the Victim position and feel the joy and delight of love emerging through you and into you and out of you into the room all around you.

And so the teacher is hating you, but you exist as love and joy, and the words that they speak to you and their rejection of you are like the words of a cartoon figure mouthing meaningless statements into space that cannot penetrate the love that you have for yourself in this moment.

And then can you take friends of yours, caregivers, parents, uncles and aunts, grandparents, cousins, siblings, picture all of them who rejected you. Line them up and see them in front of you and see your crumpled, contracted, deflated sense of longing that they love you and dissolve it completely and feel the sense that you truly do exist irrespective of who or what they are or what they think of you.

Notice how often you got angry with these people when they rejected you, but can you see that when you get angry you are fighting to reject them, but in the fighting you are locked into a dependent relationship with them. You can only feel good about yourself as long as you are fighting against them.

Now can you go beyond "existing" and feel your power, your magnificence irrespective of what others think of you, do to you.

Can you begin to discover that you are magnificent, independent of what happens in the outside world?

Independent of success, or failure, approval or rejection?

Can you feel that you are magnificent without reason, without having to search through your mind to justify this magnificence?

Can you think of something you did that you are ashamed of? Can you notice how you want to annihilate yourself? You are so ashamed that you believe you shouldn't exist. Perhaps you were laughed at or ridiculed for being stupid, nerdy, geeky, clumsy, ugly, or fat for not knowing the "right" thing to do, the right way to behave as a kid, or even as an adult.

Can you picture that behaviour and simply honour yourself in your imperfection, in not knowing what to do, what to be, to make others happy? Can you begin to celebrate your uniqueness, your individuality?

Can you love yourself even and as you break the rules, the norms, the traditions, the expectations of your culture?

*Can you begin to discover that you are magnificence, even as others **do not want you to exist, except as they dictate.***

Does that not feel amazing?

Do you not feel free?

Can you go through every person whom you can think of as having rejected you in your life and every situation which you interpreted as a sense of having failed and reclaim your sense of existence outside of that failure. This is your power.

So you've gone through everybody in your life, every event where you were dependent and come right up into the present.

Now picture all of the people in your life at the moment from whom you are deriving your sense of existence, and can you dissolve that dependency and stand in the beauty and power and love that you are, as you are?

Can you now picture the entire world shouting at you, judging you, hating you, rejecting you, trying to control you, endlessly trying to control you, and you are filled with the power and the love of yourself, for yourself, that you are?

CHAPTER 26

From Fear to Trust

The technique here is learning how to get into the energy of trust. You want to find out what trust feels like.

So, notice if you trust that the sun is going to come up tomorrow. Notice the feeling you get as you do this. Notice the sensations in the body. You are absolutely certain that it will come up, yes? Feel that certainty and the *energetic signature* of that certainty. There is an absolute knowing, a deep, wide, spacious knowing, yes?

Now think of a problem you solved easily, naturally. There was no sound on your PC and you checked the mute button. It was off and you turned it on.

So simple.

Someone came to you with a problem they wanted solved in your area of expertise and you solved it without even having to think about it.

This is trust.

Feel that energy of just knowing that all is well, it is done, no problem, no stress, no tension, just flowing into fixing.

Now think of a problem you struggled to solve, but eventually you did. You wanted to download new software on your PC and you got stuck and you couldn't fix it. And you needed help and the IT expert fixed it.

Now picture yourself being anxious before it was fixed and then bring in the energy of it being fixed into the situation, before it was fixed. You are beginning to learn to dissolve not trusting with trusting.

Now picture some problem you couldn't solve and it wasn't solved and you came to accept that this "unsolved thing" was a part of your life. My chronic fatigue issue is a great example. I have in the past been desperate to fix it and it is better than it was, but it is still an issue, yet mostly it's okay.

The okay-ness is the trust. It's okay, even though it's not so okay.

Maybe one of your kids has a learning disorder or a health issue or your partner has a health issue, or they can't make money or stay with a job or find a fulfilling career. Can you just feel the energy of trust, which says it's okay?

I mentioned earlier the families of airline accidents. Their incessant desire to know what happened, why the plan crashed, where are the bodies? Endlessly they are saying to themselves: "They have to recover the bodies. I must know what happened, why it happened!"

It drives them crazy.

Trust would say: "They are gone. It's an 'undoable' fact. Can I let go into the reality that they have passed away, that they are gone, that I have lost them? I don't need to contract emotionally into needing to know anything more."

In essence, trust is:

Embracing life's imperfections!

A FINAL NOTE

I would be delighted to assist you further in this work. Please feel free to email me with your comments, feedback or questions and go to my website for more information, subscribe to my weekly blogs and check out the Self-Esteem video course.

Email: realmark@icon.co.za
www.loveyourselffornoreason.com